THE

Witches of New York

AS ENCOUNTERED BY

Q. K. Philander Doesticks, P. B.

Preface.

What the Witches of New York City personally told me, Doesticks, you will find written in this volume, without the slightest exaggeration or perversion. I set out now with no intention of misrepresenting anything that came under my observation in collecting the material for this book, but with an honest desire to tell the simple truth about the people I encountered, and the prophecies I paid for.

So far from desiring to do any injustice to the Fortune Tellers of the Metropolis, I sincerely hope that my labors may avail something towards making their true deservings more widely appreciated, and their fitting reward more full and speedy. I am satisfied that so soon as their character is better understood, and certain peculiar features of their business more thoroughly comprehended by the public, they will meet with more attention from the dignitaries of the land than has ever before been vouchsafed them.

I thank the public for the flattering consideration paid to what I have heretofore written, and respectfully submit that if they would increase the obligation, perhaps the readiest way is to buy and read the present volume.

The Author.
Sept. 20th, 1858.

CHAPTER I.

Which is simply explanatory, so far as regards the book, butin which the author takes occasion to pay himself several merited compliments, on the score of honesty, ability, etc.

CHAPTER I.

WHICH IS MERELY EXPLANATORY.

The first undertaking of the author of these pages will be to convince his readers that he has not set about making a merely funny book, and that the subject of which he writes is one that challenges their serious and earnest attention. Whatever of humorous description may be found in the succeeding chapters, is that which grows legitimately out of certain features of the theme; for there has been no overstrained effort to *make* fun where none naturally existed.

The Witches of New York exert an influence too powerful and too wide-spread to be treated with such light regard as has been too long manifested by the community they have swindled for so many years; and it is to be desired that the day may come when they will be no longer classed with harmless mountebanks, but with dangerous criminals.

People, curious in advertisements, have often read the "Astrological" announcements of the newspapers, and have turned up their critical noses at the ungrammatical style thereof, and indulged the while in a sort of innocent wonder as to whether these transparent nets ever catch any gulls. These matter-of-fact individuals have no doubt often queried in a vague, purposeless way, if there really can be in enlightened New York any considerable number of persons who have faith in charms and love-powders, and who put their trust in the prophetic infallibility of a pack of greasy playing-cards. It may open the eyes of these innocent querists to the popularity of modern witchcraft to learn that the nineteen she-prophets who advertise in the daily journals of this city are visited every week by an average of *sixteen hundred people*, or at the rate of more than a dozen customers a day for each one; and of this immense number probably two-thirds place implicit confidence in the miserable stuff they hear and pay for.

It is also true that although a part of these visitors are ignorant servants, unfortunate girls of the town, or uneducated overgrown boys, still there are among them not a few men engaged in respectable and influential professions, and many merchants of good credit and repute, who periodically consult these women, and are actually governed by their advice in business affairs of great moment.

Carriages, attended by liveried servants, not unfrequently stop at the nearest respectable corner adjoining the abode of a notorious Fortune-Teller, while some richly-dressed but closely-veiled woman stealthily glides into the habitation of the Witch. Many ladies of wealth and social position, led by curiosity, or other motives, enter these places for the purpose of hearing their "fortunes told." When these ladies are informed of the true character of the houses they have thus entered, and the real business of many of these women whose fortune-telling is but a screen to intercept the public gaze from it, it is not likely that any one of them will ever compromise her reputation by another visit.

People who do not know anything about the subject will perhaps be surprised to hear that most of these humbug sorceresses are now, or have been in more youthful and attractive days, women of the town, and that several of their present dens are vile assignation houses; and that a number of them are professed abortionists, who do as much perhaps in the way of child-murder as others whose names have been more prominently before the world; and they will be astonished to learn that these chaste sibyls have an understood partnership with the keepers of houses of prostitution, and that the opportunities for a lucrative playing into each other's hands are constantly occurring.

The most terrible truth connected with this whole subject is the fact that the greater number of these female fortune-tellers are but doing their allotted part in a scheme by which, in this city, the wholesale seduction of ignorant, simple-hearted girls, in the lower walks of life, has been thoroughly systematized.

The fortune-teller is the only one of the organization whose operations may be known to the public; the other workers—the masculine go-betweens who lead the victims over the space intervening between her house and those of deeper shame—are kept out of sight and are unheard of. There is a straight path between these two points which is travelled every year by hundreds of betrayed young girls, who, but for the superstitious snares of the one, would never know the horrible realities of the other. The exact mode of proceeding adopted by these conspirators against virtue, the details of their plans, the various stratagems by which their victims are snared and led on to certain ruin, are not fit subjects for the present chapter; but any individual who is disposed to prosecute the inquiry for himself will find in the various police records much matter for his serious cogitation, and may there discover the exact direction in which to continue his investigations with the certainty of demonstrating these facts to his perfect satisfaction.

A few months ago, at the suggestion of the editor of one of the leading daily newspapers of America, a series of articles was written about the fortune-tellers of New York city, and these articles were in due time published in that journal, and attracted no little attention from its readers. These chapters, with such alterations as were requisite, and with many additions, form the bulk of this present volume.

The work has been conscientiously done. Every one of the fortune-tellers described herein was personally visited by the "Individual," and the predictions were carefully noted down at the time, word for word; the descriptions of the necromantic ladies and their surroundings are accurate, and can be corroborated by the hundreds who have gone over the same ground before and since. They were treated in the most fair and frank manner; the same data as to time and date of birth, age, nationality, etc., were given in all cases, and the same questions were put to all, so that the absurd differences in their statements and predictions result from the unmitigated humbug of their pretended art, and from no misinformation or misrepresentation on the part of the seeker after mystic knowledge.

This latter person was perfectly unknown to the worthy ladies of the black art profession; he was to them simply an individual, one of the many-headed public, a cash customer, who paid liberally for all he required, and who, by reason of the dollars he disbursed, was entitled to the very best witchcraft in the market.

And he got it.

He undertook a few short journeys in search of the marvellous; he went on a couple of dozen voyages of discovery without going out of sight of home; he penetrated to the out-of-the-way regions, where the two-and-sixpenny witches of our own time grow. He got his fill of the cheap prophecy of the day, and procured of the oracles in person their oracularest sayings, at the very highest market price. For the business-like seers of this age are easily moved to prophesy by the sight of current moneys of the land, no matter who presents the same; whereas the oracles of the olden time dealt only with kings and princes, and nothing less than the affairs of an entire nation, or a whole territory, served to get their slow prophetic apparatus into working trim. To the necromancers of early days the anxieties of private individuals were as naught, and from the shekels of humble life they turned them contemptuously away.

It is probably a thorough conviction of the necessity of eating and drinking, and a constant contemplation from a Penitentiary point of view of the consequences of so doing without paying therefor, that induces our modern witches to charge a specific sum for the exercise of their art, and to demand the inevitable dollar in advance.

Whatever there is of Sorcery, Astrology, Necromancy, Prophecy, Fortune-telling, and the Black Art generally, practised at this time by the professional Witches of New York, is here honestly set down.

Should any other individual become particularly interested in the subject, and desire to go back of the present record and make his exploration personally among the Fortune-tellers, he will find their present addresses in the newspapers of the day, and can easily verify what is herein written.

With these remarks as to the intention of this book, the reader is referred by the Cash Customer to the succeeding chapters for further information. And the public will find in the advertisements, appended to the name and number of each mysteriously gifted lady, the pleasing assurance that she will be happy to see, not only the Cash Customer of the present writing, but also any and all other customers, equally cash, who are willing to pay the customary cash tribute.

CHAPTER II.

Is devoted to the glorification of Madame Prewster of No. 373 Bowery, the Pioneer Witch of New York. The "Individual" also herein bears his testimony that she is oily and water-proof.

CHAPTER II.

MADAME PREWSTER, No. 373 BOWERY.

This woman is one of the most dangerous of all those in the city who are engaged in the swindling trade of Fortune Telling, and has been professionally known to the police and the public of New York for about fourteen years. The amount of evil she has accomplished in that time is incalculable, for she has been by no means idle, nor has she confined her attention even to what mischief she could work by the exercise of her pretended magic, but if the authenticity of the records may be relied on, she has borne a principal part in other illicit transactions of a much more criminal nature. She has been engaged in the "Witch" business in this city for more years than has any other one whose name is now advertised to the public.

If the history of her past life could be published, it would astound even this community, which is not wont to be startled out of its propriety by criminal development, for if justice were done, Madame Prewster would be at this time serving the State in the Penitentiary for her past misdoings; but, in some of these affairs of hers, men of so much *respectability* and political influence have been implicated, that, having sure reliance on their counsel and assistance, the Madame may be regarded as secure from punishment, even should any of her many victims choose to bring her into court.

The quality of her Witchcraft, by which she ostensibly lives, and the amount of faith to be reposed in her mystic predictions, may be seen from the history of a visit to her domicile, which is hereunto appended in the very words of the "Individual" who made it.

The "Cash Customer" makes his first Voyage in a Shower, but encounters an Oily and Waterproof Witch at the end of his Journey.

It rained, and it *meant* to rain, and it set about it with a will.

It was as if some "Union Thunderstorm Company" was just then paying its consolidated attention to the city and county of New York; or, as if some enterprising Yankee of hydraulic tendencies, had contracted for a second deluge and was hurrying up the job to get his money; or, as if the clouds were working by the job; or, as if the earth was receiving its rations of rain for the year in a solid lump; or, as if the world had made a half-turn, leaving in the clouds the ocean and rivers, and those auxiliaries to navigation were scampering back to their beds as fast as possible; or, as if there had been a scrub-race to the earth between a score or more full-grown rain storms, and they were all coming in together, neck-and-neck, at full speed.

Despite the juiciness of these opening sentences, the "Individual" does not propose to accompany the account of his heroical setting-forth on his first witch-journey with any inventory of natural scenery and phenomena, or with any interesting remarks on the wind and weather. Those who have a taste for that sort of thing will find in a modern circulating library, elaborate accounts of enough "dew-spangled grass" to make hay for an army of Nebuchadnezzars and a hundred troops of horse—of "bright-eyed daisies" and "modest violets," enough to fence all creation with a parti-colored hedge—of "early larks" and "sweet-singing nightingales," enough to make musical pot-pies and harmonious stews for twenty generations of Heliogabaluses; to say nothing of the amount of twaddle we find in American sensation books about "hawthorn hedges" and "heather bells," and similar transatlantic luxuries that don't grow in America, and never did.

And then the sunrises we're treated to, and the sunsets we're crammed with, and the "golden clouds," the "grand old woods," the "distant dim blue mountains," the "crystal lakes," the "limpid purling brooks," the "green-carpeted meadows," and the whole similar lot of affected bosh, is enough to shake the faith of a practical man in nature as a natural institution, and to make him vote her an artificial humbug.

So the voyager in pursuit of the marvellous, declines to state how high the thermometer rose or fell in the sun or in the shade, or whether the wind was east-by-north, or sou'-sou'-west by a little sou'.

The "dew on the grass" was not shining, for there was in his vicinity no dew and no grass, nor anything resembling those rural luxuries. Nor was it by any means at "early dawn;" on the contrary, if there be such a commodity in a city as "dawn," either early or late, that article had been all disposed of several hours in advance of the period at which this chapter begins.

But at midday he set forth alone to visit that prophetess of renown, Madame Prewster. He was fully prepared to encounter whatever of the diabolical machinery of the black art might be put in operation to appal his unaccustomed soul.

But as he set forth from the respectable domicile where he takes his nightly roost, it rained, as aforementioned. The driving drops had nearly drowned the sunshine, and through the sickly light that still survived, everything looked dim and spectral. Unearthly cars, drawn by ghostly horses, glided swiftly through the mist, the intangible apparitions which occupied the drivers' usual stands hailing passengers with hollow voices, and proffering, with impish finger and goblin wink, silent invitations to ride. Fantastic dogs sneaked out of sight round distant corners, or skulked miserably under phantom carts for an imaginary shelter. The rain enveloped everything with a grey veil, making all look unsubstantial and unreal; the human unfortunates who were out in the storm appeared cloudy and unsolid, as if each man had sent his shadow out to do his work and kept his substance safe at home.

The "Individual" travelled on foot, disdaining the miserable compromise of an hour's stew in a steaming car, or a prolonged shower-bath in a leaky omnibus. Being of burly figure and determined spirit, he walked, knowing that his "too-solid flesh" would not be likely "to melt, thaw, and resolve itself into a dew," and firmly believing that he was not born to be drowned.

He carried no umbrella, preferring to stand up and fight it out with the storm face to face, and because he detested a contemptible sneaking subterfuge of an umbrella, pretending to keep him dry, and all the time surreptitiously leaking small streams down the back of his neck, and filling his pockets with indigo colored puddles; and because, also, an umbrella would no more have protected a man against that storm, than a gun-cotton overcoat would have availed against the storm of fire that scorched old Sodom.

He placed his trust in a huge pair of water-proof boots, and a felt hat that shed water like a duck. He thrust his arms up to his elbows into the capacious pockets of his coat, drew his head down into the turned-up collar of that said garment, like a boy-bothered mud-turtle, and marched on.

With bowed head, set teeth, and sturdy step, the cash customer tramped along, astonishing the few pedestrians in the street by the energy and emphasis of his remarks in cases of collision, and attracting people to the windows to look at him as he splashed his way up the street. He minded them no more than he did the gentleman in the moon, but drove forward at his best speed, now breaking his shins over a dry-goods box, then knocking his head against a lamp-post; now getting a great punch in the stomach from an unexpected umbrella, then involuntarily gauging the depth of some unseen puddle, and then getting out of soundings altogether in a muddy inland sea; now swept almost off his feet by a sudden torrent of sufficient power to run a saw-mill, and only recovering himself to find that he was wrecked on the curbstone of some side street that he didn't want to go to. At length, after a host of mishaps, including som interesting but unpleasant submarine explorations in an unusually large mud-hole into which he fell full-length, he arrived, soaked and savage, at the house of Madame Prewster.

This elderly and interesting lady has long been an oily pilgrim in this vale of tears. The oldest inhabitant cannot remember the exact period when this truly great prophetess became a fixture in Gotham, and began to earn her bread and butter by fortune-telling and kindred occupations. Her unctuous countenance and pinguid form are known to hundreds on whose visiting lists her name does not conspicuously appear, and to whom, in the way of business, she has made revelations which would astonish the unsuspecting and unbelieving world. She is neither exclusive nor select in her visitors. Whoever is willing to pay the price, in good money—a point on which her regulations are stringent—may have the benefit of her skill, as may be seen by her advertisement:

"Card.—Madame Prewster returns thanks to her friends and patrons, and begs to say that, after the thousands, both in this city and Philadelphia, who have consulted her with entire satisfaction, she feels confident that in the questions of astrology, love, and law matters, and books or oracles, as relied on constantly by Napoleon, she has no equal. She will tell the name of the future husband, and also the name of her visitors. No. 373 Bowery, between Fourth and Fifth streets."

The undaunted seeker after mystic lore rang a peal on the astonished door-bell that created an instantaneous confusion of the startled inmates. There was a good deal of hustling about, and running hither, thither, and to the other place, before any one appeared; meantime, the dainty fingers of the damp customer performed other little solos on the daubed and sticky bell-pull,—and he also amused himself with inspection of, and comments on, the German-silver plate on the narrow panel, which bore the name of the illustrious female who occupied these domains.

At last the door was opened by a greasy girl, and the visitor was admitted to the hall, where he stood for a minute, like a fresh-water merman, "all dripping from the recent flood."

The juvenile female who had admitted him thus far, evidently took him for a disreputable character, and stood prepared to prevent depredations. She planted herself firmly before him in the narrow hall in an attitude of self-defence, and squaring off scientifically, demanded his business. Astrology was mentioned, whereupon the threatening fists were lowered, the saucy under-jaw was retracted, and the general air of pugnacity was subdued into a very suspicious demeanor, as if she thought he hadn't any money, and wanted to storm the castle under false pretences. She informed him that before matters went any further, he must buy tickets, which she was prepared to furnish, on receipt of a dollar and a half; he paid the money, which transaction seemed to raise him in her estimation to the level of a man who might safely be trusted where there was nothing he could steal. One fist she still kept loaded, ready to instantly repel any attack which might be suddenly made by her designing enemy, the other hand cautiously departed petticoatward, and after groping about some time in a concealed pocket, produced from the mysterious depth a card, too dirty for description, on which these words were dimly visible:

50 cents.	MADAME PREWSTER 411 Grand Street.	No. 1.

The belligerent girl then led the way through a narrow hall, up two flights of stairs into a cold room, where she desired her visitor to be seated. She then carefully locked one or two doors leading into adjoining rooms, put the keys in her pocket, and departed. Before her exit she made a sly demonstration with her fists and feet, as if she was disposed to break the truce, commence hostilities, and punch his unprotected head, without regard to the laws of honorable warfare. She departed, however, at last, without violence, though the voyager could hear her pause on each landing, probably debating whether it wasn't best after all to go back and thrash him before the opportunity was lost for ever.

This grand reception-room was an apartment about six feet by eight; it was uncarpeted, and was luxuriously furnished with six wooden chairs, one stove, with no spark of fire, one feeble table, one spittoon, and two coal-scuttles.

The view from the window was picturesque to a degree, being made up of cats, clothes-lines, chimneys, and crockery, and occasionally, when the storm lifted, a low roof near by suggested stables. The odor which filled the air had at least the merit of being powerful, and those to whose noses it was grateful, could not complain that they did not get enough of it. Description must necessarily fall far short of the reality, but if the reader will endeavor to imagine a couple of oil-mills, a Peck-slip ferry-boat, a soap-and-candle manufactory, and three or four bone-boiling establishments being simmered together over a slow fire in his immediate vicinity, he may possibly arrive at a faint and distant notion of the greasy fragrance in which the abode of Madame Prewster is immersed.

For an hour and a half by the watch of the Cash Customer (which being a cheap article, and being alike insensible to the voice of reason and the persuasions of the watchmaker, would take its own time to do its work, and the long hands of which generally succeeded in getting once round the dial in about eighty minutes) was this too damp individual incarcerated in the room by the order of the implacable Madame Prewster.

He would long before the end of that time have forfeited his dollar and a half and beaten an inglorious retreat, but that he feared an ambuscade and a pitching-into at the fair hands of the warlike servant.

Finally, this last-named individual came to the rescue, and conducted him by a circuitous route, and with half-suppressed demonstrations of animosity, to the basement. This room was evidently the kitchen, and was fitted up with the customary iron and brazen apparatus.

A feeble child, just old enough to run alone, had constructed a child's paradise in the lee of the cooking-stove, and was seated on a dinner-pot, with one foot in a saucepan; it had been playing on the wash-boiler like a drum, but was now engaged in decorating some loaves of unbaked bread with bits of charcoal and splinters from the broom.

The fighting servant retreated to the far end of the apartment, where she began to wash dishes with vindictive earnestness, stopping at short intervals to wave her dish-cloth savagely as a challenge to instant single combat. There was nothing visible that savored of astrology or magic, unless some tin candlesticks with battered rims could be cabalistically construed.

Madame Prewster, the renowned, sat majestically in a Windsor rocking-chair, extra size, with a large pillow comfortably tucked in behind her illustrious and rheumatic back. Her prophetic feet rested on a wooden stool; her oracular neck was bound with a bright-colored shawl; her necromantic locomotive apparatus was incased in a great number of predictive petticoats, and her whole aspect was portentous. She is a woman who may be of any age from 45 to 120, for her face is so oily that wrinkles won't stay in it; they slip out and leave no trace. She is an unctuous woman, with plenty of material in her—enough, in fact, for two or three. She is adipose to a degree that makes her circumference problematical, and her weight a mere matter of conjecture. Moreover, one instantly feels that she is thoroughly water-proof, and is certain that if she could be induced to shed tears, she would weep lard oil.

Grim, grizzled, and stony-eyed, is this juicy old Sibyl; and she glared fearfully on the hero with her fishy optics, until he wished he hadn't done anything.

She was evidently just out of bed, although it was long past noon, and when she yawned, which she did seven times a minute on a low average, the effect was gloomy and cavernous, and the timid delegate in search of the mysterious trembled in his boots.

At last, he with uncovered head and timid demeanor presented his card entitling him to twelve shillings' worth of witchcraft, and made an humble request to have it honored. He had previously, while pretending to warm himself at the stove, been occupied in making horrible grimaces at the baby, and then sketching it in his hat as it disfigured its own face by frantic screams; and he also took a quiet revenge on the pugnacious servant by making a picture of her in a fighting attitude, with one eye bunged and her jaw knocked round to her left ear.

When the ponderous Witch had got all ready for business, and had taken a very long greasy stare at her customer, as if she was making up her mind what sort of a customer on the whole he might be, she determined to begin her mighty magic. So she took up the cards, which were almost as greasy as she herself, and prepared for business, previously giving one most tremendous yawn, which opened her sacred jaws so wide that only a very narrow isthmus of hair behind her ears connected the top of her respected head with the back of her venerated neck.

She then presented the cards for her customer to cut, and when he had accomplished that feat, which he did in some perturbation, she ran them carelessly over between her fingers, and began to speak very slowly, and without much thought of what she was about, as if it was a lesson she had learned by heart.

Each word slipped smoothly out from her fat lips as if it had been anointed with some patent lubricator, and her speech was as follows:—

"You have seen much trouble, some of it in business, and some of it in love, but there are brighter days in store for you before long—you face up a letter—you face up love—you face up marriage—you face up a light-haired woman, with dark eyes, you think a great deal of her, and she thinks a great deal of you; but then she faces up a dark complexioned man, which is bad for you—you must take care and look out for him, for he is trying to injure you—she likes you the best, but you must look out for the man—you face up better luck in business, you face a change in your business, but be careful, or it will not bring you much money—you do not face up a great deal of money."

(Here followed a huge yawn which again nearly left the top of her head an island.) Then she resumed, "If you will tell me the number of letters in the lady's name, I will tell you what her name is."

This demand was unexpected, but her cool and collected customer replied at random, "Four." The she-Falstaff then referred to a book wherein was written a long list of names, of varying lengths from one syllable to six, and selecting the names with four letters, began to ask.

"Is it Emma?" "No." "Anna?" "No." "Ella?" "No?" "Jane?" "No." "Etta?" "No." "Lucy?" "No." "Cora?" "No." At last, finding that she would run through all the four-letter names in the language, and that he must eventually say something, he agreed to let his "true love's" name be Mary. Then she continued her remarks: "You face up Mary, you love Mary; Mary is a good girl. You will marry Mary at last; but Mary is not now here—Mary is far away; but do not fear, for you shall have Mary."

Then she proposed to tell the name of our reporter in the same mysterious manner, and on being told that it contains eight letters, the first of which is "M," she turned to her register and again began to read. It so happens that the proper names answering to the description are very few, and the right one did not happen to be on her list; so in a short time the greasy prophetess became confused, and slipped off the track entirely, and after asking about two hundred names of various dimensions, from Mark to Melchisedek, she gave it up in despair and glared on her twelve-shilling patron as if she thought he was trifling with her, and she would like to eat him up alive for his presumption.

Then she suddenly changed her mode of operation and made the fearful remark: "Now you may wish three wishes, and I will tell whether you will get them or not."

She then laid out the cards into three piles, and her visitor stated his wishes aloud, and received the gratifying information in three instalments, that he would live to be rich, to marry the light-haired maiden, and to effectually smash the dark-complexioned man.

Then she said: "You may now wish one wish in secret, and I will tell you whether you will get it." Our avaricious hero instantly wished for an enormous amount of ready money, which she kindly promised, but which he has not yet seen the color of.

He asked about his prospective wives and children, with unsatisfactory results. One wife and four children was, she said, the outside limit. At this juncture she began to wriggle uneasily in her chair, and her considerate patron respected her "rheumatics" and took his leave. This conference, although the results may be read by a glib-tongued person in five minutes, occupied more than three-quarters of an hour—Madame Prewster's diction being slow and ponderous in proportion to her size.

He now prepared to depart, and with a parting contortion of his countenance, of terrible malignity, at the unfortunate baby, which caused that weird brat to fling itself flat on its back and scream in agony of fear, he informed the Madame with mock deference that he would not wait any longer. He was then attended to the door by the bellicose maiden, who seemed to have fathomed his deep dealings with the infuriate infant, and to be desirous of giving him bloody battle in the hall, but as he had remarked that she had a rolling-pin hidden under her apron, and as he was somewhat awed by the sanguinary look of her dish-cloth, he choked down his blood-thirstiness and ingloriously retreated.

CHAPTER III.

Wherein are related divers strange things of Madame Bruce, the "Mysterious Veiled Lady," of No. 513 Broome Street.

CHAPTER III.

MADAME BRUCE, "THE MYSTERIOUS VEILED LADY," No. 513 BROOME STREET.

The woman who assumes the title of "The Mysterious Veiled Lady," is much younger in the Black Art trade than Madame Prewster, and has only been publicly known as a "Fortune-Teller" for about six years. The mysterious veil is assumed partly for the very mystery's sake, and partly to hide a countenance which some of her visitors might desire to identify on after occasions. She confines herself more exclusively to telling fortunes than do many of the others, and has never yet made her appearance in a Police Court to answer to an accusation of a grave crime. She has many customers, and might have a respectable account at the bank if she were disposed to commit her moneys to the care of those careful institutions.

It may be mentioned here, however, as a curious fact, that although all the "witches" profess to be able to "tell lucky numbers," and will at any time give a paying customer the exact figures which they are willing to prophesy will draw the capital prize in any given lottery, their skill invariably fails them when they undertake to do anything in the wheel-of-fortune way on their own individual behalf. No one of the professional fortune-tellers was ever known to draw a rich prize in a lottery, or to make a particularly lucky "hit" on a policy number, notwithstanding the fact that most of them make large investments in those uncertain financial speculations. Madame Bruce is no exception to this general rule, and the propinquity of the "lottery agency" and the "policy-shop," just round the corner, must be accepted in explanation of the fact that this gifted lady has no balance in her favor at the banker's.

The quality of her magic and other interesting facts about her are best set forth in the words of the anxious seeker after hidden lore, who paid her a visit one pleasant afternoon in August.

The "Individual" visits Madame Bruce and has a Conference with that Mysterious Veiled Personage.

A man of strong nerves can recover from the effects of a professional interview with the ponderous Prewster in about a week; delicately organized persons, particularly susceptible to supernatural influences, might be so overpowered by the manifestations of her cabalistic lore as to affect their appetites for a whole lunar month, and have bad dreams till the moon changed; but the daring traveller of this veracious history was convalescent in ten days. It is true, that, even after that time, he, in his dreams, would imagine himself engaged in protracted single combats with the heroine of the rolling-pin, and once or twice awoke in an agony of fear, under the impression that he had been worsted in the fight, and that the conquering fair one was about to cook him in a steamer, or stew him into charity soup, and season him strong with red pepper; or broil him on a gridiron and serve him up on toast to Madame Prewster, like a huge woodcock. In one gastronomic nightmare of a dream he even fancied that the triumphant maiden had tied him, hand and foot, with links of sausages, then tapped his head with an auger, screwed a brass faucet into his helpless skull, and was preparing to draw off his brains in small quantities to suit cannibalic retail customers.

But he eventually recovered his equanimity, his nocturnal visions of the warlike servant became less terrible, and he gradually ceased to think of her, except with a dim sort of half-way remembrance, as of some fearful danger, from which many years before he had been miraculously preserved.

When he had reached this state of mind, he was ready to proceed with his inquiries into the mysteries of the cheap and nasty necromancy of the day, and to encounter the rest of the fifty-cent Sybils with an unperturbed spirit. Accordingly, he girded up his loins, and prepared the necessary amount of one dollar bills; for, with a most politic and necessary carefulness, he always made his own change.

[Note of caution to the future observer of these Modern Witches: Never let one of them "break" a large bank-bill for you, and give you small notes in exchange, lest the small bills be much more badly broken than the large one. Not that the witches' money, like the fairies' gold, will be likely to turn into chips and pebbles in your pocket, but all these fortune-tellers are expert passers of counterfeit and broken bank-notes and bogus coin; and they never lose an opportunity thus to victimize a customer.]

Fortified with dinner, dessert, and cigars, the cash customer departed on his voyage of discovery in search of "Madame Bruce, The Mysterious Veiled Lady," who carries on all the business she can get by the subjoined advertisement:

"Astonishing to All.-Madame Bruce, the Mysterious Veiled Lady, can be consulted on all events of life, at No. 513 Broome st., one door from Thompson. She is a second-sight seer, and was born with a natural gift."

The "Individual," modestly speaking of himself in the third person, admits that, being then a single man of some respectability, he was at that very period looking out for a profitable partner of his bosom, sorrows, joys, and expenses. He naturally preferred one who could do something towards taking a share of the expensive responsibility of a family off his hands, and was not disposed to object to one who was even afflicted with money;—next to that woman, whom he had not yet discovered, a lady with a "natural gift" for money-making was evidently the most eligible of matrimonial speculations. Whether he really cherished an humble hope that the veil of Madame Bruce might be of semi-transparent stuff, and that she might discover and be smitten by his manly charms, and ask his hand in marriage, and eventually bear him away, a blushing husband, to the altar, or whatever might be hastily substituted for that connubial convenience, will never be officially known to the world. Certain it is that he expected great results of some sort to eventuate from his visit to this obnubilated prophetess, and that he paid extraordinary attention to the decoration of the external homo, and to the administration of encouraging stimuli to the inner individual, probably with a view to submerge, for the time, his characteristic bashfulness, before he set out to visit the fair inscrutable of Broome-street.

The nature of his secret cogitations, as he walked along, was somewhat as follows, though he himself has never before revealed the same to mortal man.

He was of course uncertain as to her personal attractiveness; owing to that mysterious veil there was a doubt as to her surpassing beauty. At any rate he did not regret the time spent on his toilet.

Madame Bruce might be a lady of the most transcendent loveliness, or she might possess a countenance after the style of Mokanna, the Veiled Prophet; in either case, a clean shirt collar and a little extra polish on the boots would be a touching tribute of respect. He thought over the stories of the Oriental ladies, so charmingly and complexly described in the "Arabian Nights' Entertainments," and in some strange way he connected Madame Bruce with Eastern associations; he remembered that in Asiatic countries the arts of enchantment are the staple of fashionable female education; that the women imbibe the elements of magic from their wet nurses, and that their power of charming is gradually and surely developed by years and competent instructors, until they are able to go forth into the world, and raise the devil on their own hook.

In this case the veil was of the East, Eastern; and what was more probable than that the "Mysterious Veiled Lady" was that fascinating Oriental young woman whose attainments in magic made her the dire terror of her enemies, most of whom she changed into pigs, and oxen, and monkeys, and other useful domestic animals; who had transformed her unruly grandfather into a cat of the species called Tom; had metamorphosed her vicious aunt into a screech-owl, and had turned an ungentlemanly second-cousin into a one-eyed donkey.

What a treasure, thought the "Individual," would such an accomplished wife be in republican America,—how exceedingly useful in the case of her husband's rivals for Custom-house honors, and how invaluable when creditors become clamorous. What a perfect treasure would a wife be who could turn a clamorous butcher into spring lamb, and his brown apron and leather breeches into the indispensable peas and mint-sauce to eat him with; who could make the rascally baker instantly become a green parrot with only power to say, "Pretty Polly wants a cracker;" who could transform the dunning tailor into a greater goose than any in his own shop; who could go to Stewart's, buy a couple of thousands of dollars' worth of goods, and then turn the clerks into cockroaches, and scrunch them with her little gaiter if they interfered with her walking off with the plunder; or who, in the event of a scarcity of money, could invite a select party of fifty or sixty friends to a nice little dinner, and then change the whole lot into lions, tigers, giraffes, elephants, and ostriches, and sell the entire batch to Van Amburgh & Co. at a high premium, as a freshly imported menagerie, all very fat and valuable.

Then he came down from this rather elevated flight of fancy, and filled away on another tack. Before he reached the house he had fully made up his mind that Madame Bruce, the Mysterious Veiled Lady, must be a stray Oriental Princess in reduced circumstances, cruelly thrust from the paternal mansion by the infuriated proprietor, her father, and compelled to seek her fortune in a strange land. He had never seen a princess, and he resolved to treat this one with all respect and loyal veneration; to do this, if possible, without compromising his conscience as a republican and a voter in the tenth ward,—but to do it at all hazards.

The immense fortune which would undoubtedly be hers in the event of the relenting of her brutal though opulent father, suggested the feasibility of a future elopement, and a legal marriage, according to the forms of any country that she preferred—he couldn't bethink him of a Persian justice of the peace, but he did not despair of being able to manage it to her entire and perfect satisfaction.

Her undoubted great misfortunes had touched his tender heart. He would see this suffering Princess— he would tender his sympathy and offer his hand and the fortune he hoped she would be able to make for him. If this was haughtily declined there would still remain the poor privilege of buying a dose of magic, paying the price in current money, and letting her make her own change.

Having matured this disinterested resolve, he proceeded calmly on his journey, wondering as he walked along, whether, in the event of a gracious reception by his Princess, it would be more courtly and correct to kneel on both knees, or to make an Oriental cushion of his overcoat and sit down cross-legged on the floor.

This knotty point was not settled to his entire satisfaction when he reached that lovely portion of fairy-land near the angle of Broome and Thompson streets. The Princess had taken up her temporary residence in the tenant-house No. 513 Broome, which, elegant mansion affords a refuge to about seventeen other families, mostly Hibernian, without very high pretensions to aristocracy.

His ring at the door of the noble mansion was answered by a grizzly woman speaking French very badly broken, in fact irreparably fractured. This grizzly Gaul let him into the house, heard his request to see Madame Bruce, and then she called to a shock-headed boy who was looking over the bannisters, to come and take the visitor in charge.

Two minutes' observation convinced the distinguished caller that the servants of the Princess were not particular in the matter of dirt.

The walls were stained, discolored, and bedaubed, and the floor had a sufficient thickness of soil for a vegetable garden; at one end of the hall, indeed, an Irish woman was on her knees, making experimental excavations, possibly with a view to planting early lettuce and peppergrass.

A glance at the shock-headed boy showed a peculiarity in his visual organs; his eyes, which were black naturally, had evidently suffered in some kind of a fisticuff demonstration, and one of them still showed the marks; it was twice black, naturally and artificially; it had a dual nigritude, and might, perhaps, be called a double-barrelled black eye. This pleasant young man conducted his visitor to the top of the first flight of stairs, where he said, "Please stop here a minute," and disappeared into the Princess's room, leaving her devoted slave alone in the hall with two aged washtubs and a battered broom. There ensued an immediate flurry in the rooms of the Princess, and the customer thought of the forty black slaves, with jars of jewels on their heads, who, in Oriental countries, are in the habit of receiving princesses' visitors with all the honors. He hardly thought to see the forty black slaves, with the jars of gems, but rather expected the shock-headed youth to presently reappear, with a mug of rubies, or a kettle of sapphires and emeralds, and invite him in courtly language to help himself to a few—or, that that active young man would presently come out with an amethyst snuff-box full of diamond-dust and ask him to take a pinch, and then present him with that expensive article as a slight token of respect from the Princess.

"Not so, not so, my child."

The great shuffling and pitching about of things continued, as if the furniture had been indulging in an extemporaneous jig, and couldn't stop on so short a notice, or else objected to any interruption of the festivities.

Finally the rattling of chairs and tables subsided into a calm, and the boy reappeared. He came, however, without the tea-kettle full of valuables, and minus even the snuff-box; he merely remarked, with an insinuating wink of the lightest-colored eye, "Please to walk this way."

It *did* please his auditor to walk in the designated direction, and he entered the room, when the eye spoke again to a very low accompaniment of the voice, as if he was afraid he might damage that organ by playing on it too loudly.

The anxious visitor looked for the Princess, but not seeing her, or the slaves with the pots of jewels, and observing, also, that the chairs were not too luxuriously gorgeous for people to sit on, he sat down.

A single glance convinced him that the Princess could have had no opportunity to carry off her jewels from her eastern home, or that she must have spent the proceeds before she furnished her present domicile. An iron bedstead, a small cooking-stove, four chairs, and a table, on which the breakfast crockery stood unwashed, was the amount of the furniture. A dirty slatternly young woman of about twenty-three years, with filthy hands and uncombed hair, and whose clothes looked as if they had been tossed on with a pitchfork, seated herself in one of the chairs and commenced conversation—not in Persian. It was one o'clock, P.M., but she attempted an apology for the unmade bed, the unswept room, the unwashed breakfast dishes, and the untidy appearance of everything. Before she had concluded her fruitless explanation, the boy with the variegated eye suddenly came from a closet which the customer had not noticed and was unprepared for, and said, in winning tones, "Please to walk in this room," which was done, with some fear and no little trembling, whereupon the optical youth incontinently vanished.

At last, then, the imaginative visitor stood in the presence of royalty, and beheld the wronged Princess of his heart. He was about to drop on his bended knees to pay his premeditated homage, but a hurried glance at the floor showed that such a course of proceeding would result in the ineffaceable soiling of his best pantaloons; so he stood sturdily erect.

Before he suffered his eyes to rest upon the peerless beauty who, he was convinced, stood before him, he took a survey of the regal apartment.

An unpainted pine table stood in the corner, a gaudily colored shade was at the window, and an iron single bedstead upon which the clothes had been hastily "spread up," and two chairs, on one of which sat the enchantress, completed the list.

The Princess was attired in deep black, and a thick black veil, reaching from her head to her waist, entirely concealed her features from the beholders who still devoutly believed in her royal birth and cruel misfortunes—nor was this belief dissipated until she spoke; but when she called "Pete" to the double-barrelled youth with the eye, and gave him a "blowing up" in the most emphatic kind of English for not bringing her pocket-handkerchief, then the beautiful Princess of his imagination vanished into the thinnest kind of air, and there remained only the unromantic reality of a very vulgar woman, in a very dirty dress, and who had a very bad cold in her head. There was still a hope that she might be pretty, and her would-be admirer fervently trusted that she might be compelled to lift her veil to blow her nose, but she didn't do it. Then he offered her his hand, not in marriage, but for her to read his fortune in, and stood, no longer trembling with expectation, but with stony indifference, for as he approached her, a strong odor of an onion-laden breath from beneath the veil, gave the death-blow to the fair creature of his imagination, and convinced him that he had got the wrong —— Princess by the fist. She looked at him closely for a couple of minutes, and then spoke these words—the peculiar pronunciation being probably induced by the cold in her head.

"You are a badd who has saw a great beddy chadges add it seebs here as if you was goidg to be bore settled in the future—it seebs here like as if you had sobetibes in your life beed very buch cast dowd, but it seebs here like as if you had always got up agaid.—It seebs here like as if you had saw id your past life sobe lady what you liked very buch add had beed disappointed—it seebs here like as if there was two barriages for you, wud id a very short tibe—wud lady seebs here to stadd very dear to you, add you two bay be barried or you bay dot—if you are dot already barried you will be very sood—it seebs here as if you woulddt have a very large fabily—five childred will be all that you will have—you will have a good deal of buddy (money) id your life—sobe of your relatives what you dever have saw will sood die add leave you sobe property—but you will dot be expectidg it add it seebs here as if you would have trouble id getting it, for there will sobe wud else try to get it away frob you—it seebs as if the lady you will barry will dot be too dark cobplexiod, dor yet too light—dot too tall, dor yet very short, dot too large, dor too thid—she thidks a great deal of you, bore thad you do of her,—you have already saw her id the course of your life, and she loves you very buch. There are people about you id your busidess who are dot so buch your friends as they preted to be—you are goidg to bake sub chadge id your busidess, it will be a good thidg for you add will cub out buch better thad you expect."

Here she stopped and intimated that she would answer any questions that her customer desired to ask, and in reply to his interrogatories the following important information was elicited:

"You will be lodg lived, add you will have two wives, add will live beddy years with your first wife."

The "Individual" proclaimed himself satisfied, and paid his money, whereupon Madame Bruce instantly yelled "Pete," when the Eye-Boy reappeared to show the door, and the Cash Customer departed, leaving the Mysterious Veiled Lady shivering on her stool, and exceedingly desirous of an opportunity to use her pocket-handkerchief.

And this is all there was of the Persian Princess. As the seeker after wisdom went away he made one single audible remark by way of consoling himself for his crushed hopes and blighted anonymous love. It was to this effect. "I believe she squints, and I *know* she's got bad teeth."

CHAPTER IV.

Relates the marvellous performances of Madame Widger, of No. 3, First Avenue, and how she looks into the future through a Paving-Stone.

CHAPTER IV.

MADAME WIDGER, No. 3 FIRST AVENUE.

Madame Widger came from Albany to this city about four years ago, and at once set up as an "Astrologer." She has been a "witch" for a great many years, and has, directly and indirectly, done about as much mischief as it is possible for one person to accomplish in the same length of time. She was a woman of great repute in and about Albany, as a fortune-teller, and was supposed to be conversant with practices more criminal. She at last became so well known as a bad woman, that she found it advisable to leave Albany, after she had settled certain lawsuits in which she had become entangled.

Among other speculations of hers, in that place, she once sued the city to recover indemnifying moneys for certain imaginary damages, alleged to have been done to her property by the unbidden entrance of the river into her private apartments, during one of the periodical inundations with which Albany is favored. By the shrewd management of certain of her lawyer friends with whom she had business dealings, she at last got a judgment against the city, but, owing to some other awkward law complications, it became expedient to change her place of residence before she had collected her money, and the amount remains unpaid to this day.

She then came to this city, and set up in the Sorceress way, and, by dint of advertising, she soon got a good many customers. She now has as much to do as she can easily manage to get along with, is making a good deal of money by "Astrology," and by other more unscrupulous means; and she is probably worth some considerable property. She is a bold, brazen, ignorant, unscrupulous, dangerous woman. She has some peculiar ways of her own in telling the fortunes of her visitors, and is the only person in the city who professes to read the future through a magic stone, or "second-sight pebble." Her manner of using this wonderful geological specimen is fully described hereafter.

The "Individual" Visits a Grim Witch, who reads his Future through a Moderate-Sized Paving-Stone.

Disappointed in his fond hope of discovering, in the person of Madame Bruce, an eligible partner, who should bridal him and lead him coyly to the altar, that bourne from which no bachelor returns, the Cash Customer was for many days downcast in his demeanor and neglectful of his person. When he eventually recovered from his strong attack of Madame Bruce, he was not by any means cured of his romantic desire to procure a witch wife. He had carefully figured up the conveniences of such an article, and the sum total was an irresistible argument.

If he could win a witch of the right sort, perhaps she could teach him the secret of the Philosopher's Stone, and the Elixir of Life, and show him the locality of the Fountain of Youth, so that he could take the wrinkles out of himself and his friends, at the cost of only a short journey by rail-road. A barrel or so of that wonderful water, peddled out by the bottle, would meet a readier sale and pay a larger profit than any Paphian Lotion that was ever advertised on the rocks of Jersey. All this, to say nothing of a family of young wizards and sorcerers, who could, by virtue of the maternal magic, swallow swords from the day of their birth, do mighty feats of legerdemain, such as cutting off the heads of innumerable pigs and chickens, and producing the decapitated animals alive again from the coat-tails of the bystanders, to the astonishment of the crowd and the great emolument of their proud dad. Even if these profitable babies should not be natural necromancers, with the power of second sight, and any quantity of "natural gifts," they must surely be spirit-rappers of the most lucrative "sphere," capable of organizing "circles," and instructing "mediums," and otherwise bringing into the family fund large piles of that circulating medium so much to be desired. Or, even failing this popular gift, they *must* all be born with some strong instincts of money-making vagabondism. If the girls failed in fortune-telling they would certainly have a genius for the tight-rope, or a decided talent for the female circus and negro-minstrel business; and the boys would be brought into the world with the power of throwing a miraculous number of consecutive flip-flaps—of putting cocked hats on their juvenile heads while turning somersets over long rows of Arab steeds of the desert—of poising their infant bodies on pyramids of bottles, and drinking glasses of molasses and water, under the contemptible subterfuge of wine, to the health of the terror-stricken beholders—or of climbing to the tops of very tall poles without soiling their spangled dresses, and there displaying their anatomy for the admiration of the gazing multitude, in divers attitudes, for the most part extraordinarily wrong side up with very particular care—or, at least, they would be born with the astounding gift of tying their young legs in double bow-knots across the backs of their adolescent necks, and while in that graceful position kissing their little fingers to the bewildered audience.

Under the constant influence of such comfortable and ennobling thoughts, it is not in the elastic nature of the human mind to remain long dejected. In the contemplation of the future glories of his might-be wife and possible family, the "Individual" recovered somewhat of his former gaiety. Remembering that "Care killed a cat," he resolved that he would not be chronicled as a second victim, so he kicked Care out of doors, so to speak, and warned Despair and Discouragement off the premises.

He attired him in his best, and appeared once more before the world in the joyful garb of a man with Hope in his heart and money in his pantaloons. In fact, so radiant did he appear, that he might have been set down for a person who had just had a new main of joy laid on in his heart, and had turned the cocks of all the pipes, and let on the full head just to see how the new apparatus worked. Or, as if he'd been in a shower-bath of good-nature, and come out dripping.

He also took kindly to that innocuous beverage, lager bier, which was a good sign in itself, inasmuch as he had, for a few days, been drinking as many varieties of strong drinks, as if he'd been brought up on Professor Anderson's Inexhaustible Bottle, and had never overcome the influences of his infant education.

Seeking out a friend to whom he confided his hopes of a lucrative wife and a profitable progeny, the Cash Customer suggested that they proceed immediately in search of the fair enchantress who was to be his comfort and consolation, for the rest of his respectable life.

Being somewhat disgusted with the result of his visit to the witch with the romantic designation of the "Mysterious Veiled Lady," he had determined to seek out one on this occasion with the most common-place and every-day cognomen, in the whole list. There being a Madame Widger in that delightful catalogue, of course Widger was the one selected. It is true, she sometimes advertised herself as the "Mysterious Spanish Lady," but in the judgment of the Individual, the Widger was too much for the Spanish and the mystery.

So Madame Widger was resolved on. Her modest advertisement is given, that the impartial reader may be brought to acknowledge that the inducements to wed the Widger were not of the common order.

"Madame Widger, the Natural-Gifted Astrologist, Second-Sight Seer and Doctress, tells past, present, and future events; love, courtship, marriage, absent friends, sickness; prescribes medicines for all diseases, property lost or stolen, at No. 3 First-av., near Houston-st."

The slight lack of perspicuity in this announcement seems to be a mysterious peculiarity, common to all the Fortune Tellers, as if they were all imbued with the same commendable contempt for all the rules of English grammar.

The voyager being attired in a captivating costume, and being also provided with pencils and paper to make a life-sketch, with a view to an expansive portrait of his enslaver, whose beauty was with him a foregone conclusion, set out with his faithful friend for the delightful locality mentioned in the advertisement, where the charming Circe, Widger, held her magic court.

He was not aware, at that time, that his intended bride was not a blushing blooming maiden, but an ancient dame, whose very wrinkles date back into the eighteenth century. But of that hereafter.

He was determined to have her tell his "love, courtship, or marriage, absent friends, or sickness," and to insist that she should "prescribe medicines for property lost or stolen," according to the exact wording of the advertisement.

The doughty "Individual" trembled somewhat, with an undefined sensation of awe, as though some fearful ordeal was before him—to use his own elegant and forcible language, he felt as though he was going to encounter an earthquake with volcano trimmings.

"It is the fluttering of new-born love in your manly bosom," remarked his companion.

"Well," was the reply, "if a baby love kicks so very like a horse of vicious propensities, a full-grown Cupid would be so unmanageable as to defy the very Rarey and all his works."

Without any noteworthy adventure they kept on their way to the First Avenue, and in due time stood, awe-struck, before the mansion of the enchantress.

After the first impression had worn off, the scene was somewhat stripped of its mysteriousness, and assumed an aspect commonplace, not to say seedy. As soon as the sense of bewilderment with which they at first gazed upon the domicile of the mysterious damsel so favored of the fates, had passed away, they found themselves in a condition to make the observations of the place and its surroundings that are detailed below.

The house, a three-story brick, seemed to have that architectural disease which is a perpetual epidemic among the tenant-houses of the city, and which makes them look as if they had all been dipped in a strong solution of something that had taken the skin off. The paint was blistered and peeling off in flakes; the blinds were hanging cornerwise by solitary hinges; the shingles were starting from their places with a strange air of disquietude, as if some mighty hand had stroked them the wrong way; the door-steps were shaky and crazy in the knees; the door itself had a curious air of debility and emaciation, and the bell-knob was too weak to return to its place after it had feebly done its brazen duty. There was no door-plate, but on a battered tin sign was blazoned, in fat letters, the mystic word "Widger." The Cash Customer rang the bell, not once merely, or twice, but continuously, in pursuance of a dogma which he laid down as follows:

"It is a mistake to ever stop ringing till somebody comes. The feebler you ring, the more the servants think you're a dun, and therefore the more they don't come to let you in—but if you keep it up regularly they'll think you're a rich relation and will rush to the rescue."

So he kept on, and the voice of the bell sharply clattered through the dismal old house, making as much noise as if it suddenly wakened a thousand echoes that had been locked up there for many years without the power to speak till now. If a timid ring denotes a dun, and a boisterous one a rich relation, then must the inhabitants of that cleanly suburb have been convinced that the present performer on the bell not only had no claims as a creditor on the people of the house, but was a rich California uncle, come to give each adult member of that happy family a gold mine or so, and to distribute a cart-load of diamonds among the children.

The door at last was opened by an uncertain old man with very weak eyes, who appeared to have, in a milder form, the same malady which afflicted the house; perhaps he was a twin, and suffered from brotherly sympathy—at any rate the dilapidating disease had touched him sorely; its ravages were particularly noticeable in the toes of his boots and the elbows of his coat. Violent remedies had evidently been applied in the latter case, but the patches were of different colors, and suggestive of the rag-bag; the boots were past hope of convalescence; his shirt-collar was sunk under a greasy billow of a neckcloth, and only one slender string was visible to show where it had gone down; the nether garment was a ragged wreck, that set a hundred tattered sails to every breeze, but was anchored fast at the shoulder with a single disreputable suspender.

Guided by this equivocal individual the two visitors entered a small shabbily furnished room, and bestowed themselves in a couple of treacherous chairs, in pursuance of an imbecile invitation from the battered old gentleman.

The anticipations of the enthusiastic lover again began to fall, and in five minutes his heart, which so lately was "burning with high hope," was so cold as to be uncomfortable.

On a seven-by-nine cooking-stove, which three pints of coal would have driven blazing crazy, stood a diminutive iron kettle, in which something was noisily stewing; the something may have been a decoction of magic herbs, or it may have been Madame Widger's dinner. A tumble-down trunk in a corner of the room did precarious duty for a chair; a faded carpet hid the floor; a cheap rocking-chair in the act of moulting its upholstery spread its luxurious arms invitingly near the dim window; and a table, on which a pack of German playing cards was coyly half concealed by a newspaper, a coal-hod, and a poker, completed the necessary furnishing of the apartment.

The ornaments are soon inventoried; a certificate of membership of the New York State Agricultural Society, given at Albany to Mr. M. G. Bivins, hung in a cheap frame over the table. The other decorations were a few prints of high-colored saints, an engraving of a purple Virgin Mary with a pea-green child, and a picture of a blue Joseph being sold by yellow brethren to a crowd of scarlet merchants who were paying for him with money that looked like peppermint lozenges.

Madame Widger, the "Mysterious Spanish Lady," was not at first visible to the naked eye, but a loud, shrill, vicious voice, which made itself heard through the partition dividing the reception-room from some apartment as yet unexplored by them, directed the attention of her visitors to her exact locality.

She was "engaged" with another gentleman, said the knight of the ragged inexpressibles.

Had not what he had already seen of the mansion decidedly cooled the passion of the love-lorn customer, this intelligence would have been likely to rouse his ire against the interloping swain, and make him pant for vengeance and fistic damages to the other party; but in his present confused state of mind he received this blow with philosophic indifference.

The old man subsided into a chair, and in a weak sort of way began to talk, evidently with some insane idea of pleasingly filling up the time until the prophetess should be disengaged. His conversation seemed to run to disasters, with a particular partiality to shipwrecks. He accordingly detailed, with wonderful exactness, the perils encountered by a certain canal-boat of his, "loaded principally with butter and cheese," during a dangerous voyage from Albany to New York, and which was finally brought safely to a secure harbor by the power of the Widger, which circumstance had made him her slave for life.

The shrill voice then ceased, and the person to whom it had been addressed came forth. The lime on his blue jean garments, and the cloudy appearance of his boots, declared him to be something in the mason line. He deported himself with becoming reverence, and departed in apparent awe. He did not look like a dangerous rival, and he was not molested.

A discreditable and disordered head now thrust itself out of the mysterious closet, opened its mouth, and the vicious voice said: "I will see you now, sir." The sighing swain, with a fluttering heart and unsteady steps, summoned his courage and entered the place, to him as mysterious as was Bluebeard's golden-keyed closet to his ninth wife. The first glance at Madame Widger at once scattered again all his dreams of love and of happiness with that potent and fearful female.

He encountered a cadaverous bony-looking woman, very tall, very old, though with hair still black; with grey eyes, and false gleaming teeth. She was attired in calico; quality, ten cents a yard; appearance, dirty. Hardly was the door closed, when the vicious voice spitefully remarked, "Sit down, sir;" and a skinny finger pointed to a cane-bottomed chair. While seating himself and taking off his gloves, he took an observation.

The apartment was not large; in an unfurnished state, a moderately-hooped belle might have stood in it without serious damage to her outskirts, but there would be little extra room for any enterprising adventurer to circumnavigate her. In one corner was a small pine light-stand, on which was a sceptical looking Bible, with a very black brass key tied in it; a volume of Cowper bound in full calf; a little lamp with a single lighted wick, and a pile of the Madame's business hand-bills.

She at once showed her experience of human nature and her distrust of her present visitor by her practical and matter-of-fact conduct.

She sat uncomfortably down on the very edge of an angular chair, folded her hands, shut herself half up like a jack-knife, and the vicious voice mentioned this fearful fact: "My terms are a dollar for gentlemen;" and the grey eyes stonily stared until the dollar aforesaid was produced.

The voice then prepared for business by sundry "Ahems!" and when fairly in working order it proceeded: "Give me your hand—your *left* hand."

The Widger took the extended palm in her shrivelled fingers and made four rapid dabs in the middle of it with the forefinger of her other hand, as if she were scornfully pointing out defects in its workmanship; then she opened the drawer of the little stand with a spiteful jerk, and withdrew thence something which she put to her sinister optic, and began rapidly screwing it round with both hands, as if she had got water on the brain and was trying to tap herself in the eye.

Then the vicious voice began, in a loud mechanical manner, to speak with the greatest volubility, running the sentences together, and not thinking of a comma or a period till her breath was exhausted, in a manner that would have fairly distanced Susan Nipper herself, even if that rapid young lady had twenty seconds the start.

"I see by looking in this stone that you was born under two planets one is the planet Mars you will die under the planet Jupiter but it won't be this year or next you have seen a great deal of trouble and misfortune in your past life but better days are surely in store for you you have passed through many things which if written in a book would make a most interesting volume I see by looking more closely in the stone that you are about to receive two letters one a business letter the other a let—"

Here her breath failed, and as soon as it came back the voice continued —

"ter from a friend it is written very closely and is crossed I see by looking more closely in the stone that one of the letters will contain news which will distress you exceedingly for a little while but you need not be troubled for it will all be for your good you are soon to have an interview with a man of light hair and blue eyes who will profess great interest in you but he will get the advantage of you if he can you must beware of him I see by looking more closely in the stone that you will live to be 68 years old but you will die before you are 70." Here was another station where the locomotive voice stopped to take in air, and then instantly dashed ahead at a greater speed than ever. "I see by looking more closely in the stone that good luck will befall you a near friend will die and leave you a fortune I see by looking more closely in the stone that this will happen to you when you are between 32 and 34 years old that is all I see in this stone."

Another grab brought from the little drawer another pebble, which the Madame placed at her eye, the boring operation was recommenced, and the vicious voice once more got up steam.

"I see by looking closely in this stone that you will have two wives one will be blue-eyed and the other will be black-eyed with the first one you will not live long but with the last one you will be happy many years I see by looking more closely in the stone that you will have six children which will be very comfortable the lady who is to be your first wife is at this moment thinking of you I see by looking more closely in the stone that a man with light hair and blue eyes is trying to get her away from you but she scorns him and turns away I see by looking more closely in the stone that she has a strong feeling for you you need not fear the man with light hair and blue eyes for you will get her you and you only will possess her heart I see by looking more closely in the stone that she is good gentle kind loving affectionate true-hearted and pleasant."

(The vicious voice resented each one of these good-natured adjectives, as if it had been a gross personal insult to the Widger, and spit them spitefully at her trembling customer, as if they tasted badly in her mouth.)

"and will make you a good wife; you will be rich and happy you will be successful in business you will be hereafter always lucky you will be distinguished you will be eminent you will be good you will be respected you will be beloved honored cherished and will reach a good old age I see by looking in this stone—that is all I see by looking in this stone."

Here she ceased, and choking down her indignation, which had risen to a fearful pitch during the complimentary peroration, she said, taking up the equivocal Bible with the key tied in it, "Take hold of the key with your finger, I will give you one wish, if the book turns round you will have your wish." The guest took the key in the required manner, and the Widger closed her eyes and muttered something which may have been either a prayer or a recipe for pickling red cabbage, for he was unable to satisfy himself with any degree of certainty what it was; at the appointed time the book turned and the wish was therefore graciously granted.

Her hearer smiled his grimmest smile, and ventured to inquire if his unknown rival was making any progress in securing the affections of the lady in dispute, and received the satisfying answer, "She scorns him and turns away." Reassured by this, the susceptible individual mentally and fiercely defied the blue-eyed intruder to do his worst, and with a reverential obeisance left the presence. As he departed, the skinny hand presented him with a handbill, but the vicious voice was silent.

Carefully conning the handbill as they slowly departed from the august realm of the Madame, the seekers of magic for the lowest cash price read the following particulars:

"Madame Widger was born with this wonderful gift of revealing the destinies of man, and she has revealed mysteries that no mortal knew. She states that she advertises nothing but what she can do with entire satisfaction to all who wish to consult her.

"Also, she will scan aright, Dreams and visions of the night."

The tender inquirer went away in a desponding mood. The Widger was out of the question as a bride, "for she was old enough," he said, "to have been grandmother to his father's uncle."

CHAPTER V.

Discourses of Mrs. Pugh, of No. 102 South First Street, Williamsburgh, and tells all that Nursing Sorceress communicated to her Cash Customer.

CHAPTER V.

MRS. PUGH, No. 102 SOUTH FIRST STREET, WILLIAMSBURGH.

It is travelling a little away from home to go to Williamsburgh in search of a witch, but there are some peculiar circumstances about the present case, that give it more than common interest. Mrs. Pugh is not an *advertising* sorceress, but practises all her magic slily, and generally under a promise of secresy, which is exacted lest the fame of her fortune-telling should come to the ears of certain respectable families, who employ her as a nurse. She is much resorted to by a number of young persons of both sexes, and has considerable notoriety among the low and ignorant classes as a practiser of the black art. She is by no means the only "nurse" who is given to this reprehensible practice, but very many of the old women who officiate as professional nurses are proficients in telling fortunes with cards, and with the Bible and key, and are always glad of an opportunity to exhibit their pretended skill. Being at times received into families where there are daughters, not grown up, they become most dangerous persons if they are encouraged or permitted to thus practise on the credulity of these young girls.

The mere encouragement of hurtful superstitious notions is a great ill in itself, but is by no means the extent of the evil done by some of these persons. They not unfrequently take an active part in bringing about meetings between unsuspecting girls and evil-disposed men, thus paving the way to the wretchedness and ruin of the former. More than one instance is known, where the going astray of a loved daughter can be traced directly to the mischievous teachings of a fortune-telling nurse.

These are the reasons that give the case of Mrs. Pugh an importance greater than attaches to many others.

It is right that people should know that a certain degree of circumspection ought to be used, with regard to moral character, as well as other qualifications, in the selection of a nurse, lest a person be employed who will work irreparable mischief among the younger members of the family.

The Individual calls on a Nursing Sorceress.

Who shall say that broomstick locomotion is a lost art, and that steam has superseded magic in the matter of travelling? Because no one of us has ever encountered a witch on her basswood steed, shall we presume to assert that witches no longer bestride basswood steeds and make their nocturnal excursions to blasted heaths, there to meet the devil in the social midnight orgie, and kick up their withered heels in the gay diabolical dance with other ancient females of like kidney with themselves? Because no one of us has ever beheld with his own personal optics, an old woman change herself into a black cat, shall we therefore assert that the ancient dames of our own day are unable to accomplish that feline transformation? "Not by no manner of means whatsomdever," as Mr. Weller would remark.

Let us not then be found without charity for the peculiar and persistent faith of the hero of this book, who, though thrice bitterly disappointed in his matrimonial speculations among the witches, still clung to the fond belief that a bride with supernatural powers of doing things would be a splendid speculation, and that such a spouse could be found if he, her ardent lover, did not give up the chase too soon. Spite of his disappointment with Madame Bruce, and his crushing discomfiture with Madame Widger, Hope still sprang eternal in the "Individual's" breast, and he felt, like the immortal Mr. Brown of classic verse, that it would "never do to give it up so."

He had something of a natural turn for mechanics, and having been of late engaged in some entertaining speculations on steam engines, he came not unnaturally to think of the wonderful advantage the magically-endowed people of old had over the present age in the matter of locomotion. He thought of that wonderful carpet on which a jolly little party had but to seat themselves and wish to be transported to any far-off spot, and presto! change! there they were instanter. No collisions to be feared; no running off the track at a speed of ever-so-many unaccountable miles an hour; no cast-iron-voiced conductor at short intervals demanding tickets; no old women with sour babies; no obtrusive boys with double-priced books and magazines; no other boys with peanuts, apples, and pop-corn; nothing, in fact, save one's own social circle but a civil genie, not of Irish extraction, to fly alongside to mix the juleps and carry the morning paper.

It was very natural to consider whether there wasn't a yard or two left somewhere of that valuable carpet, and to regret that on the whole probably the original owners had occasion to use the entire piece.

Then the thought was very naturally suggested of the marvellous wooden horse with the pegs in his neck, who soared with his riders a great deal higher than does Mr. Wise in his clumsy balloon, and always came down a great deal easier than ever Mr. Wise did yet. Of course the Cash Customer was from the start perfectly convinced that *that* breed of horses is long since extinct, so long ago that no record of them is now to be found in either the "American Racing Calendar," or the "English Stud Book."

Then very naturally came thoughts of the broomstick changes of the more modern witches. Perhaps, he thought, these are the colts of the wooden horse, degenerate, it is true, and lacking in the grace and symmetry of their extraordinary sire, but still perhaps not inferior in speed or in safety of carriage.

The thought was a brilliant one, and it was really worth while to inquire into the matter and pursue this phantom steed until he was fairly hunted down and bridled ready for use.

It needed no long cogitation or extended argument to convince Johannes, the "Individual," the Cash Customer, of the immense practical value of such a steed, to say nothing of his costing nothing to keep, and of its therefore being utterly impossible for him to "eat his own head off," and of his never growing old, and of his never having any of the multitudinous diseases that afflict ordinary horses without any intermixture of magic blood, and therefore of it being out of the question for anybody to cheat his owner in a horse-trade.

Why, only think of his value for livery purposes in case his happy proprietor was disposed to let other folks use him for a proper compensation. He could of course be trained to carry double, and no doubt Mr. Rarey, or some other person potent in horse education, could easily break him to go in harness.

It wasn't likely, Johannes cogitated, that the judges would allow him to enter his ligneous racer at the Fashion Course, so that he'd not get a chance to win any money from Lancet and Flora Temple, still there was a hope, even on that point.

So, in search of the witch wife, whose dower should be the broomstick horse, that should set the fond couple up in business, started the sanguine lover.

Having had some experience of New York fortune-tellers and others in the magic line, and not thinking they were of the sort likely to have so great a treasure, he started for the suburbs, and crossed the ferry to Williamsburgh, in order to pay a visit of inquiry, and if possible to take the initiatory step in courting Mrs. Pugh, of No. 102 South First Street, in that city.

He designed, of course, to buy a "fortune" at a liberal price, for the purpose of setting the lady in good-humor as a necessary preliminary step. He really had hopes that she would prove to be of a slightly different style from some of the New York fortune-tellers, who seem to have mistaken their profession and to be hardly up to reading the stars with success, although they might be fully equal to all the financial exigencies of an apple and peanut stand, or might win an honorable distinction crying "radishes and lettuce" in the early morning hours; or upon trial, might, perhaps, evince a decided genius for the rag-picking business, or preside over the fortunes of a soap-fat cart with distinguished ability.

Threading the winding ways of Williamsburgh is by no means an easy task for one unaccustomed, and it was only by incessantly stopping the passers-by and making the most minute inquiries that this lady was ever achieved at all.

This constant questioning of the public revealed, however, the fact that Mrs. Pugh does not by any means depend upon her fortune-telling for her bread-and-butter; she is a nurse, as many a Williamsburgh baby could testify if it could command its emotions long enough to speak. What will be the influence of her supernaturalism and witchcraft upon the children intrusted to her fostering care—whether they will in after life prove to be devils, demi-gods, heroes, or mere ordinary "humans," time alone can show. This illustrious lady does not advertise in the newspapers; in fact, her fortune-telling is done on the sly, as if she were yet an apprentice, and a little ashamed of her bungling jobs, for which, by the way, she only charges half price. She is in a very undecided state, and evidently undetermined whether her proper vocation is tending babies or revealing the decrees of the fates at twenty-five cents a head, and when her visitors made their appearance she was puzzled to know whether their business was baby or black art.

Her exertions in either profession have not as yet gained her a very large fortune, judging from the surroundings of her eligible residence.

The domicile of this chrysalis enchantress is a low frame house of two stories, standing back from the street, directly in the rear of another row of more pretentious mansions, as if it had been sent into the back yard in disgrace and never permitted to show itself in good society again. It seems conscious of its humiliation, and wears an air of architectural dejection that is quite touching. A troop of dirty-faced children was in the yard, and in the corner was a pile of other household incumbrances, consisting principally of mops and washtubs.

Johannes critically examined this interesting collection, but the wished-for broomstick was not there. A modest rap brought to the door a large ill-favored man with a red nose and a ponderous pair of boots, whose speciality seemed to be drinking whatever spirituous liquors were consumed about the establishment.

Having passed this shirt-sleeved sentinel without damage, though not without fear, the Cash Customer sat down to take an observation.

The wooden courser was not to be seen at first glance. The room was a small irregularly-shaped one, with an intrusive chimney jutting out into the floor from one side, as if it were a sturdy brick-and-mortar poor relation of the premises come a visiting and not to be got rid of at any price. A small cooking-stove was in the fireplace, with an attendant on either side in the shape of a battered coal-scuttle, and a small saucepan full of charcoal; the floor was covered with a dirty rag carpet that had long since outlived its beauty and its usefulness, and was now in the last extremity of a tattered old age; half-a-dozen chairs of different patterns, all much shattered in health and enfeebled by long years of labor, and a decrepit lounge in the last stages of a decline, were the seats reserved for visitors; the other furniture of the room was an antique chest of drawers of a most curious and complicated pattern—it seemed as if the mechanic had been uncertain whether he was to construct a bureau or a cow-shed, and had accordingly satisfied his conscience by making half-a-dozen drawers and building a sloping roof over them; the joints were warped apart, and through the chinks could be seen fragments of clean shirt, and ends of lace, and bits of flannel, suggesting babies. At a wink from the female, the male with the ponderous boots retired from the presence.

Mrs. Pugh is a woman of medium height and size, with a clear grey eye, and light hair, and wearing that sycophantic smile peculiar to people who have much to do with ugly babies whose beauty must be constantly praised to the doting parents. She was attired in a neat calico dress, constructed for family use, and for the particular accommodation of the younger members of the household.

Johannes, who had been taking a sly look, had made up his mind that she would not be quite so objectionable for a wife as he had feared, and he had fully resolved to woo and wed her off-hand, provided she had the broomstick of his hopes.

So, by way of a beginning, he announced that he would like her to exercise her magic powers in his behalf.

Mrs. Pugh had evidently previously regarded him as an enthusiastic young father with a pair of troublesome twins, who had come to seek her ministrations, and she undoubtedly had high wages, innumerable presents, and exorbitant perquisites in her mind's eye at that instant.

When, however, she learned that her visitor merely wished to know what the fates had resolved to do about his particular case, she was slightly disappointed, for the babies are more profitable than the planets. However, she soon reconciled herself to her fate, and produced from some cranny immediately under the eaves of the cow-shed bureau, a pack of cards wrapped up in an old newspaper. She then carefully locked the door to keep out the children, and drew down the curtains lest their inquiring minds should lead them to observe her mysterious operations through the window. Then taking the wonder-working pieces of pasteboard in her hands, and seating herself opposite her visitor, she announced her gracious will, thus: "You shall have six wishes."

Then, without asking him what he wished for, or whether he wished for anything, she shuffled the cards a few seconds, and read off their mysterious significance as follows, her curious and anxious customer looking furtively around, meanwhile, to spy out the hiding-place of the wooden courser:

"'Pears to me you will have good luck in futur, though it seems to me that you have had a great deal of bad luck and misfortune in your life; but you will certainly do better in your futur days than you have done yet in your life, at least, so it seems to me. 'Pears to me your good luck will commence right away, pretty soon, immediate, in a very few days; you will have some great good luck befal you within a 9. I designate time by days, and weeks, and months, and sometimes years, so this good luck of which I told you, you will certainly have within 9 days, or 9 weeks, or 9 months, or possibly 9 years—9 days I think; yes, I am sure; within 9 days, at least so it 'pears to me. You are going to make a change in your business, so it seems to me—you are going to leave your present business, and make a change; you will make this change within a 7, which may be 7 days or weeks; weeks I think, yes certainly within 7 weeks, at least so it 'pears to me—this change in your business which will take place in 7 days, or weeks, I think, yes weeks I'm sure, will be a change for the better, and you will profit by it much, at least so it seems to me—and it will come to pass within a 7; as I said before, within a 7, months or days it may be, but weeks I think; yes, now I look again, within a 7, weeks I'm certain, at least, so it 'pears to me—you will receive a letter within a 3; years, perhaps, months, it may be, but still it looks like days; yes, days I'm sure, days it must be; within a 3, and days they are; you will receive a letter within 3 days, I'm positively sure, or so it 'pears to me. You have friends across water, from whom you will hear speedily and soon, within a 5, which may be months, although I think not, for it looks like years; did I say years? no, days; yes, days it is again; within a 5, and days they are; this letter you will have within 5 days; it will contain excellent news, which will please you much; money, the news will be, and you will get the letter within a 5, which may be months or years, but days it looks like, and first-rate news it is, of money; I am positively certain that it is within a 5, at least it seems so to me. You face up good luck and prosperity, and you will be very rich before you die, though I do not see how you are to get your money, whether by business or legacy; but you will be very rich, or so it seems to me. You will receive some money within a 4; it will be in three parcels, and there will be considerable of it. You will get it in three parcels within a 4, not hours, nor years, nor yet months, but weeks; money in three parcels within a 4, and weeks they are, I'm certain. The money will be in three parcels—three parcels; in three parcels you will get money within a 4, which, now I look again, it may be years, but still I think not. No, it is weeks; I'm certain, at least, so it 'pears to me. There is a lady that has a good heart for you. She is a light-complexioned lady, with black eyes; she has a good heart for you, and I do not see any trouble between you, which means that there is no opposition to your match, and that you will certainly marry her within a 2, at least so it 'pears to me. Within a 2 you will marry this light-complexioned lady, within a 2, which is not hours, nor yet days, I think it is months. I'll look again; no, it is not months, but years; within a 2 and years they are, yes, 2 years; before a 2, and years they are, this lady will be your wife—at least, so it seems to me. 'Pears to me you will get money with her, I do not know how much, but you will certainly get money in three parcels, as I once remarked before, within a 4, which I'm sure is weeks. You will be married twice; once within a 2, once again within a 5 or 7 after your first wife dies. I think it is a 5, though it may be a 7; and months it looks like, though it may be weeks or days. You will live with your first wife a 10; days it can't be, though it looks like days—a 10, you'll live with her a 10, can it be hours, no, years it is, it must be, because you will have five children by your first wife, which makes it years—10 years it is, I know, at least so it 'pears to me. You will have five children by your first wife, but you will not raise them all. All will die but two, and then your wife will die within a 1, which is a month, or so it seems to me."

The inquirer was charmed with the lively prospect of so many funerals, and mentally resolved to buy a couple of acres in Greenwood for the accommodation of his future family. His meditations were interrupted by the lady, who thus continued:

"You will marry a second wife, but you will have trouble about her; there is a dark-complexioned man who interferes, and who will trouble you for an 8, which may be years, although I think not, nor hours, nor days, but months; I'm sure it is—yes, the dark-complexioned man will trouble you for an 8, which I am sure is months, yes, months it is, an 8 I say, and months they are, I am certain, at least so it 'pears to me. By your second wife you will have three children, who will all live—I see a funeral here within a 6; it does not look like a friend or a relative, but it is some acquaintance, or the friend of some acquaintance, or the acquaintance of some friend—the funeral is within a 6, but it does not come very near to you—you will go to a wedding within a 3, and you will receive a present of a ring within a 2, which may be days—you will after this be very prosperous and happy, you will be very long-lived—you will get a letter and a present from the light-complexioned lady within a 9, which, as I said before, it may be hours, which I think it is, though weeks it may be, or months, or even years; though certainly within a 9, which, now I look again, is days, yes, I am sure, certain, within a 9, a letter and a present from the light-complexioned lady, a 9 it is and days, within a 9, and days they are, at least, so it 'pears to me."

Here ended the communication, and, on inquiring the price, Johannes was astonished to learn that he had received but twenty-five cents' worth. Regretting that he had not invested a dollar in a commodity so "cheap and very filling at the price" for future consumption, he departed, first taking a long lingering look to find, if possible, the lurking-place of the magic broomstick charger. He didn't see it, and gave it up, and came away declaring that such a woman was not qualified to take the social position his wife must assume. He did not, however, wish to discourage her; he thought that the water-melon trade might be comprehended by a lady of her abilities, or that she could perhaps thoroughly master the pop-corn and molasses candy business, and make it lucrative.

CHAPTER VI.

In which are narrated the Wonderful Workings of Madame Morrow, the "Astonisher," of No. 76. Broome Street; and how, by a Crinolinic Stratagem, the "Individual" got a Sight of his "Future Husband."

CHAPTER VI.

MADAME MORROW, THE ASTONISHER, No. 76 BROOME STREET.

Madame Morrow is the only one of the fortune-telling fraternity in New York who refuses to dispense her astrological favors to both sexes. She positively declines receiving any visits from "gentlemen," and confines her business attention exclusively to "ladies," of whom many are her regular customers. One reason for this course of conduct is, that she imagines her own sex to be the more credulous, and more readily disposed to put faith in her claims to supernatural knowledge, and she naturally prefers to deal with believers rather than with sceptics. Her "lady" customers are more tractable and easily managed than men, and are not so apt to ask puzzling and impertinent questions; and as the Madame can manage more of them in a day, of course the pecuniary return is larger than if she exercised her art in behalf of curious masculinity as well.

Of her history before she engaged in her present business, not much is known to those who have met her only of late years, for with regard to her early life she chooses to exercise a politic reticence. The whole "style" of the woman, however, her dress, manner, and conversation, are strong indications that her younger and more attractive days were not passed in a nunnery, but more probably in establishments where "Free Love" is more than a theory. The character of the greater part of her "lady" visitors is of a grade that goes to corroborate this supposition, and leads to the belief that among women of doubtful virtue "old acquaintance" is not easily "forgot." By far the greater number of Madame Morrow's customers are girls of the town, and women of even more disreputable character.

The fact that a visit to this renowned sorceress must be paid in a feminine disguise, made the attempt to secure an interview of more than ordinary interest. How this difficulty was mastered, and how an entrance was finally effected into the citadel from which all mankind is rigorously excluded, is best told in the words of the "Individual" who accomplished that curious feat.

How the Cash Customer visited the "Astonisher"—How he was Astonished—and How he saw his Future Husband.

The Cash Customer in pursuit of a wife had been rebuffed, but was not disheartened. He had, so to speak, fought a number of very severe hymeneal rounds and got the worst of them all; but he had taken his punishment like a man, and had still wind and pluck to come up bravely to the matrimonial scratch when "time" was called, and as yet showed no signs of giving in. His backers, if he'd had any, would have still been tolerably sure of their money, and not painfully anxious to hedge. The bets would have been about even that he'd win the fight yet, and come out of the battle a triumphant husband, instead of being knocked out of the field a disconsolate and discomfited bachelor.

But, although his ardor had not cooled, and though his strength and determination still held out, he had grown slightly cautious, and had conceived a plan for going like a spy into the camp of the enemy, and there thoroughly reconnoitring the positions that he had to storm, and at the same time making himself master of the wiles and stratagems that were the peculiar weapons of the female foe, and so learn some infallible way to capture a first-quality wife. At any rate, he would give himself the benefit of the doubt and make the experiment. He would a-wooing go, not apparelled in conquering broadcloth, in subjugating marseilles, or overpowering doeskin, but carrying the unaccustomed, but not less potent weapons of laces, moire-antique, crinoline, and gaiters.

In fact, there was also a stern necessity in the case, for the lady on whom he had now set his young affections was particular as to her customers, and did not admit the shirt-collar gender to the honor of her confidence.

But was this to stop him? If the lady shut out the whole masculine world from the inevitable fascinations of her superabundant charms, was it not for sweet charity's sake, that a whole community might not go into ecstatic frenzies over her peerless beauty, and all men, being stricken in love of the same woman, go to cutting each other's throats with bowie-knives and other modern improvements!

It was easy to see that *Madame Morrow* did not want to become another Helen, to be abducted to some modern Troy, and have a ten years' row, and any quantity of habeas corpuses, and innumerable contempts of interminable courts, after the modern fashion of conducting a strife about a runaway maiden.

Such a considerate beauty, veiling her undoubted fascinations from the rude gaze of man, from purely prudential reasons, must be a prize of rare value, and well worth the winning.

Her qualifications in magic, too, seemed to be of the very first order, to judge from her notification to the wonder-seeking world.

"Astonishing to All.—Madame Morrow claims to be the most wonderful astrologer in the world, or that has ever been known, as I am the seventh daughter of the seventh daughter, who was also a great astrologist. I have a natural gift to tell past, present, and future events of life. I have astonished thousands during my travels in Europe. I will tell how many times you are to be married, how soon, and will show you the likeness of your future husband, and will cause you to be speedily married, and you will enjoy the greatest happiness of matrimonial bliss and good luck through your whole life. I will also show the likeness of absent friends and relations, and I will tell so true all the concerns of life that you cannot help being astonished. No charge, if not satisfied. Gentlemen not admitted. No. 76 Broome street, near Columbia."

There was but one thing in this that troubled the "Individual" with any particularly sharp pangs. He intended to marry the Astonisher, but he was a little bothered what to do with the seven daughters, for of course the Madame would not fail to follow the excellent example of her revered mother, and would never stop short of the mystic number.

He finally concluded that all his duties as a father would be faithfully performed if he taught them to read, write, and play on the piano, and then gave them each a sewing-machine to begin the world with. He did think of bringing them up for the ballet, but their success in that profession being somewhat dependent on the size and symmetry of their dancing implements, he felt it would be improper to positively determine on that line of business before he had been favored with a sight of the young ladies. Reserving, therefore, his decision on this knotty point until time should further develop the subject, he prepared for the unsexing which was indicated as an inevitable preliminary to a visit to Madame Morrow, by the sentence "Gentlemen not admitted."

He proposed to get himself up in a way that would slightly astonish the Madame herself, although she had faithfully promised in her advertisement to astonish him. He would have been willing to wager a small sum that with all her witchcraft she would be unable to keep that promise, for in the regular course of his business, he had become so accustomed to marvels, wonders, and miracles, that the upheaval of a volcano in the Park wouldn't discompose him unless it singed his whiskers. He had a strong desire, however, to realize the old sensation of astonishment, and he was of the opinion that the "likeness of his future husband" would accomplish that feat if anything could.

Heroic was Johannes, and withal ingenious, and this then was his wonderful plan.

He would visit this Madame Morrow, not by proxy, but in his own proper person; if not as a man, then as a woman; yes, he would petticoat himself up to the required dimensions, if it took a week to tie on the machinery. Off with the pantaloons; on with the skirts; down with the broadcloth; hurrah for the cotton and hey for victory, and a look at his future husband.

To an inventor of theatrical costumes hied he with this fell design in his heart.

The requisite paraphernalia were bargained for and sent home to the ambitious voyager, who, at the sight thereof, was "astonished" in advance, and stricken aghast by the complicated mysteries of laces, ribbons, strings, bones, buttons, pins, capes, collars, and other inexplicable articles that met his gaze.

The question instantly occurred, "Could he get into these things?"

Not a bit of it; he would sooner undertake to report in short-hand the speech of a thunder-cloud, and with much better prospects of success. He felt his own insignificance, and as he looked out at the window, he regarded a passing female with awe. He felt that he was fast becoming imbecile, not to say idiotic, when he bethought him of his friends. Two discreet married men, who knew the ropes, were called to the rescue, and began the work; they piled on layer after layer of the material, and in the course of four or five hours had built him into a pyramid of the proper size, when they gave him their solemn assurance that he was "all right." He has since discovered that they had tied his undersleeves round his ankles, and that the things he wore on his arms must have belonged somewhere else. There was trouble about the hair, and it required the combined ingenuity and wisdom of the masculine trio to keep the bonnet on, and this difficulty was only overcome at last by tying strings from the inside of the crown of that invention to the ears of the sufferer.

Then, and not till then, had anybody thought of the whiskers. They must be sacrificed; and though the miserable victim to his own ambition consented to the disfigurement, how was it to be accomplished? The luckless Johannes could no more sit down in a barber's chair than the City Hall could get into an omnibus. At last he knelt down, which was the nearest approach he could make to a sitting position, and Jenkins, mounted on the bed, shaved him as well as he could at arm's length.

When the operation was concluded, his head looked as if it had been parboiled and the skin taken off. He didn't dare to curse Jenkins for his clumsiness, knowing that if he relieved his mind in that desirable manner, Jenkins would refuse to help him undress when he wanted to get out of the innumerable manacles that now confined every joint. He was as helpless as a turtle that the unkind hand of ruthless man has rolled over on his back.

However, the disguise was complete; he looked in the glass and thought he was his own landlady; his best friends wouldn't have known him, and the teller of the bank would have pronounced him a forgery and refused to certify him; he felt like a full-rigged clipper ship, and got under sail as soon as possible and bore down upon Madame Morrow's residence. He nearly capsized as he stepped into the street, but he righted after a heavy lurch to the north-east, and kept his course without further serious disaster. He made a speedy run to Broome street, the voyage being accomplished in less than the expected time, although a heavy sea, in the shape of a boy with a wheelbarrow, struck him amidships, on the corner of Sheriff street, doing some damage to his lower works and carrying away a yard or so of lace from his main skirt. He finally came up to the house in splendid style, and cast anchor on the opposite sidewalk to take an observation.

The anchorage was good, and he rode securely for a short time until he could repair damages, he having carried away some of his upper rigging; in other words, he had caught his veil on a meat-hook and had been unable to rescue it. He rigged a sort of jury-veil with the end of his shawl, so that he could hide his blushing countenance in case of too close scrutiny.

Madame Morrow lives, as he now discovered, in a low, three-story brick house, which cannot be called dirty, simply because that mild word expresses an approximation towards cleanliness which no house in this locality has known for years. City readers can get an idea of its condition by understanding that it is in the worst part of "The Hook;" to readers in the country, who have luckily never seen anything filthier than a barn yard, no information can be given which would meet the case. Sunshine is the only protection for a well-dressed man against the population of this part of the town. In the twilight or darkness he would be robbed, if not garroted and murdered. The boldest and most desperate burglars, and others of that stamp, have their homes about here—fathers who teach their children the thief's profession, and mothers who carry pickpockets at the breast. In the midst of this nest of crime the fortune-teller has her home, and here she thrives.

The daring man, protected by his false colors, there being no officious authority in that neighborhood to exercise the right of search, came alongside the house and prepared, metaphorically, to board; that is, he rang the bell.

He was admitted by an Irish girl, whose incrusted face showed that the same deposit of dirt had probably held possession undisturbed for weeks. They had just entered the hall door when two small children, who were contending for their vested rights with a big yellow dog that had interfered with their dinner, commenced an unearthly squalling, which, for the instant, made the millinery delegate fairly believe that Tophet was out for noon. The Hibernian maiden, with great presence of mind, immediately attempted to quiet the storm by administering to each inverted brat a sound correction, in the manner usually adopted by mothers.

Particulars are omitted.

Then she resumed her attentions to the stranger, and convoyed him into port in the parlor. Securely harbored in this safe retreat, Johannes took another observation.

The room was small, and what few things were in it looked shabby and dirty of course. The principal article of furniture was a huge basketful of soiled linen, which had probably been "taken in" to wash, and from a respectable family, for every single article looked ashamed to be caught in such company, and tried to burrow down out of sight. Disconsolate shirts elbowed humiliated socks, which in turn kicked against mortified flannels, or hid themselves beneath disconcerted sheets; abashed shirt-collars and humbled dickies tried to shrink out of sight in very shame beneath a dishonored tablecloth, the wine-stains on which showed it to belong in better society. A dejected and cast-down woman was assorting the despairing contents of the basket with a look of desolation.

The girl, who had disappeared, now returned, and with an air of mystery slipped into the hand of her visitor a red card, on which was inscribed:

No Person allowed to remain in the Establishment without a ticket. Please present this on entering Madame Morrow's room. Fee in full, $1.

For an hour and a half after the receipt of this card and the payment of $1 therefor, did Johannes quietly wait in the room with the big basket, being entertained meanwhile by the two women who conversed with each other upon the relative merits of engines No. 18 and 27, and with a long discussion as to the comparative personal beauty of "Tom" and "Dick," who, it seemed, belonged respectively to those two mechanical constituents of our Fire Department.

At the end of that time the Irish girl, who had succeeded in establishing "Dick's" claim to her satisfaction, arose and invited the stranger to the room of Madame Morrow.

He passed up a narrow flight of stairs, the condition of which, as to dirt, was concealed by no friendly carpet; then he sailed into a front parlor which was furnished elegantly, and perhaps gorgeously, with carpets, mirrors, sofas, and all the usual requirements of a lady's apartment.

Madame herself appeared at the door. She is a tall, sallow-looking woman, with a complexion the color of old parchment: with light brown eyes and light hair; being attired in a handsome delaine dress of half-mourning, and decorated with a costly cameo pin and ear-drops, she looked not unlike a servant out for a holiday, making a sensation in her mistress's finery.

She led her lovely visitor into a little closet-like room, in which were a bureau, two chairs, a table, and a small stand, covered with a number of her business hand-bills and a pack of cards. She asked first: "What month was you born?" On receiving the answer, the Astonisher took a book from the bureau and read as follows: "A person born in this month is of an amiable and frank disposition, benevolent, and an amiable and desirable partner in the marriage relation. Your lucky days are Tuesdays and Thursdays, on which days you may enter on any undertaking, or attempt any enterprise with a good prospect of success." Then she took up the cards again, and after the usual shuffling and cutting, the Astonisher fired away as follows.

"You face luck, you face prosperity, you face true love and disinterested affection, you face a speedy marriage, you face a letter which will come in three days and will contain pleasant news—you face a ring, you face a present of jewelry done up in a small package; the latter will come within two hours, two days, two weeks, or two months—you face an agreeable surprise, you face the death of a friend, you face the seven of clubs which is the luckiest card in the pack—you face two gentlemen with a view to matrimony, one of whom has brown hair and brown eyes, and the other has lighter hair and blue eyes—they are both thinking of you at the present time, but the nearest one you face is the one with light eyes— your marriage runs within six or nine months."

There was very much more to the same effect, but as Johannes was pining all this time for a look at his future husband, he did not pay the strictest attention to it. Finally, when she had finished talking, she said, "Step this way and see your future husband."

This was the eventful moment.

The disguised one went to the table and there beheld a pine box, about the size of an ordinary candle-box, though shallower; it was unpainted, and decidedly unornamental as an article of furniture. In one end of it was an aperture about the size of the eye-hole of a telescope; this was carefully covered with a small black curtain. This mystic contrivance was placed upon a table so low that the husband-seeker was compelled to go on his knees to get his eye down low enough to see through. He accomplished this feat without grumbling, although his knees were scarified by the whalebones which surrounded him. The Astonisher then drew aside the little curtain with a grand flourish, and her customer beheld an indistinct figure of a bloated face with a mustache, with black eyes and black hair; it was a hang-dog, thief-like face, and one that he would not have passed in the street without involuntarily putting his hands on his pockets to assure himself that all was right. But he felt that he had no hope of a future husband if he did not accept this one, and he made up his mind to be reconciled to the match.

This contrivance for showing the "future husband" is sometimes called the Magic Mirror, and may be procured at any optician's for a dollar and a quarter. The "future husband" may of course be varied to suit circumstances, by merely shifting the pictures at one end of the instrument; or a horse or a dog might be substituted with equal propriety and probability.

Disappointed, and sick at heart and stomach, the Cash Customer bore away for home, and accomplished the return voyage without disaster. He didn't so much mind the unexpected difference in the personal attractions of Madame Morrow from what he had hoped, for he had been rather accustomed to disappointments of that sort of late, but he couldn't see that his admission to the camp of the enemy had enabled him to spy out anything of particular advantage to him in future operations. So he cogitated and mournfully whistled slow tunes, as he cut himself out of his unaccustomed harness by the help of a pen-knife with a file-blade.

CHAPTER VII.

Contains a full account of the interview of the Cash Customer with Doctor Wilson, the Astrologer, of No. 172 Delancey Street. The Fates decree that he shall "pizon his first Wife." Hooray!!

CHAPTER VII.

DR. WILSON, No. 172 DELANCEY STREET.

This ignorant, half-imbecile old man is the only *wizard* in New York whose fame has become public. There are several other men who sometimes, as a matter of favor to a curious friend, exercise their astrological skill, but they do not profess witchcraft as a means of living; they do not advertise their gifts, but only dabble in necromancy in an amateur way, more as a means of amusement than for any other purpose. On the other hand Dr. Wilson freely uses the newspapers to announce to the public his star-reading ability, and his willingness, for a consideration, to tell all events, past and future, of a paying customer's life. He professes to do all his fortune-telling in a "strictly scientific" manner, and it is but justice to him to say, that he alone, of all the witches of New York, drew a horoscope, consulted books of magic, made intricate mathematical calculations, and made a show of being scientific. In his case only was any attempt made to convince the seeker after hidden wisdom, that modern fortune-telling is aught else than very lame and shabby guesswork. The old Doctor has by no means so many customers as many of his female rivals; he is old and unprepossessing—were he young and handsome the case might be otherwise.

He has been a pretended "botanic physician," or what country people term a "root doctor;" but failing to earn a living by the practice of medicine, he took up "Demonology and Witchcraft" to aid him to eke out a scanty subsistence. He does but little in either branch of his business, the public appearing to have slight faith in his ability either to cure their maladies or foretell their future.

The character of his surroundings is noted in the following description, and his oracular communication is given, word for word.

An Hour with a Wizard.—The Cash Customer is to "Pizon" his First Wife, and then get Another. Hooray!

"I am like a vagabond pig with no family ties, who has no lady pig to welcome him home o'nights, and with no tender sucklings to call him 'papa,' in that prattling porcine language that must fall so sweetly on the ears of all parents of innocent porklings. Like Othello, I have no wife, and really I can see little hope in the future."

Thus moralized the "Individual," the morning after his experiment with the women's gear, and his failure to learn, at a single lesson, the whole art of catching a wife. Then he bethought him that perhaps the art could not be learned without a master; and then came the other thought that no one could tell so well how to win a witch-wife as one who had himself been successful in that risky experiment.

To find a man with a fortune-telling wife is no easy matter, for most of the marriages contracted by these ladies are by no means of a permanent character, and the male parties to the temporary partnerships are always kept in the background. But if he could discover up a wizard, a masculine master of the Black Art, there were strong probabilities that such an individual could put him in the way of winning a miracle-working spouse, at the very least possible trouble and expense. He would seek that man as a preliminary to winning that woman. The daily newspapers showed him that in the person of a learned doctor, surnamed Wilson, he would probably find the man he wanted. He searched out that wonderful man, and the results of his visit are given in this identical chapter.

Old dreamy Sol Gills, of coffee-colored memory, has been admiringly recommended to the good opinion of the world by his friend, Capt. Ed'ard Cuttle, mariner of England, as a man "chock full of science." From the same eminent authority we also learn that Jack Bunsby was an individual of learning so vast, and experience so varied and comprehensive, that he never opened his oracular mouth but out fell "solid chunks of wisdom." That the person now dwells in our city who combines the scientific attainments of Gills with the intuitive wisdom of Bunsby, we have the solemn word of

Johannes. The science is a trifle more dreamy and misty even than of old, and the wisdom is solider and chunkier, but both are as undeniable, as convincing, as "stunning," as in the best days of the Little Wooden Midshipman. The fortunate possessor of this inestimable wealth of knowledge secludes himself from the curious public in the basement of the house No. 172 Delancey street, like an underground hermit. However, this unselfish and generous sage, not wishing to hide entirely the light of his great learning from a benighted world, kindly condescends, in the advertisement herewith given, to retail his wisdom to anxious inquirers at a dollar a chunk:

"Astrology.—Dr. Wilson, 172 Delancey street, gives the most scientific and reliable information to be found on all concerns of life, past, present, and future. Terms—ladies, 50 cents; gentlemen, $1. Birth required."

The last sentence is slightly obscure, and it was not quite clear to Johannes that he would not have to be "born again" on the premises. But at all events there was something refreshing in the novelty of consulting a "learned pundit" in pantaloons, after all the tough conjurers of the other sex that he had undergone of late.

So he repaired to Delancey street in a joyous mood, nothing daunted by the requirements of the advertisement.

Delancey street is not Paradise, quite the contrary. In fact it may be set down as unsavory, not to say dirty in the extreme. The man that can walk through the east end of this delicious thoroughfare without a constant sensation of sea-sickness, has a stomach that would be true to him in a dissecting-room. The individual that can explore with his unwilling boots its slimy depths without a feeling of the most intense disgust for everything in the city and of the city, ought to live in Delancey street and buy his provisions at the corner grocery. He never ought to see the country, or even to smell the breath of a country cow. He should be exiled to the city; be banished to perpetual bricks and mortar; be condemned to a never-ending series of omnibus rides, and to innumerable varieties of short change.

The delegate picked his way gingerly enough, thinking all the while that if Leander had been compelled to wade through Delancey street, instead of taking a clean swim across the sea, Hero might have died a respectable old maid for all Leander. And yet Johannes says he doesn't believe that History will give *him* any credit for his valorous navigation of the said street.

He at last reached the designated spot, sound as to body, though wofully soiled as to garments, and approached the semi-subterranean abode of the great prophet, and immediately after his modest rap at the basement door, was met by the venerable sage in person. He walked in, and then proceeded to take an observation of the cabalistic instruments and mysterious surroundings of the great philosopher.

The room was a small, low apartment, about ten feet by twelve, the floor uncarpeted and uneven; the walls were damp, and the whole place was like a vault. The furniture was very scanty, and all had an unwholesome moisture about it, and a curious odor, as if it gathered unhealthy dews by being kept underground. Three feeble chairs were all the seats, and a table which leaned against the wall was too ill and rickety to do its intended duty; many of the books which had once probably covered it, were now thrown in a promiscuous heap on the floor, where they slowly mildewed and gave out a graveyard smell. A miniature stove in the middle of the room, sweated and sweltered, and in its struggles to warm the unhealthy atmosphere had succeeded in suffusing itself with a clammy perspiration; it was in the last stages of debility; old age and abuse had used it sadly, and it now stood helplessly upon its crippled legs, and supported its nerveless elbow upon a sturdy whitewash brush. There were a few symptoms of medical pretensions in the shape of some vials, and bottles of drugs, and colored liquids on the mantelpiece; a great attempt at a display of scientific apparatus began and ended with an insulating stool, and an old-fashioned "cylinder and cushion" electrical machine; a number of highly-colored prints of animals pasted on the wall, having evidently been scissored from the show-bill of a menagerie, had a look towards natural history, and a jar or two of acids suggested chemical researches. The books that still remained on the enervated table were an odd volume of Braithwaite's Retrospect, a treatise on Human Physiology, and another on Materia Medica; a number of bound volumes of Zadkiel's Astronomical Ephemeris, Raphael's Prophetic Almanac, Raphael's Prophetic

Messenger, and a file of Robert White's Celestial Atlas, running back to 1808.

The appearance of the venerable sage of Delancey street was not so imposing as to strike a stranger with awe—quite the contrary. He partook of the character of the room, and was a fitting occupant of such a place; he seemed some kind of unwholesome vegetable that had found that noisome atmosphere congenial, and had sprung indigenously from the slimy soil. One looked instinctively at his feet to see what kind of roots he had, and then glanced back at his head as if it were a huge bud, and about to blossom into some unhealthy flower. The traces of its earthy origin were plainly visible about this mouldy old plant; quantities of the rank soil still adhered to the face, filled up the wrinkles of the cheeks, found ample lodging in the ears and on the neck, and crowding under the horny and distorted nails, made them still more ugly; and streaks and ridges of dirt clung to every portion of the garments, which answered to the bark or rind of this perspiring herb.

To drop this botanic figure of speech, Dr. Wilson is a man of about fifty-eight years of age, rather stout and thick-set, with grey eyes, and hair which was once brown, but is now grey, and with thin brown whiskers; the top of his head is nearly bald, except a few thin, furzy, short hairs, which made his skull look as if it had been kept in that damp room until mould had gathered on it. He was in his shirt sleeves, and was attired, for the most part, in a pair of sheep's grey pantaloons, which were made to cover that fraction of his body between his ankles and his armpits; the little patch of shirt that was visible above the waistband of that garment, was streaked with irregular lines of dirty black, as if it had gone into half mourning for the scarcity of water.

The man of science made a musty remark or two about the weather and the walking, and then, after carefully seating himself at the decrepit table, he said: "I suppose your business is of a fortun'-tellin' natur; if so, my terms is one dollar." The affirmative answer to the question and the payment of the dollar put new energy into the mouldy old man, and he prepared to astonish the beholder.

He demanded the age of his visitor, and then desired to be informed of the date of his birth, with particular reference to the exact time of day; Johannes drummed up his youthful recollections of that interesting event, and gave the day, the hour, and the minute, with his accustomed accuracy. The sage made an exact minute of these wet-nurse items on a cheap slate with a stub of a pencil; then taking another cheap slate, he proceeded to draw a horoscope thereon, pausing a little over the signs of the zodiac, as if he was a little out in his astronomy, and wasn't exactly certain whether there should be twelve or twenty. He settled this little matter by filling one half the slate as full as it would hold, and then carrying some to the other side, so as to have a few on hand in case of any emergency.

When the figure was drawn, and all the mysterious signs completed, the shirt-sleeve prophet became absorbed in an intricate calculation of such mysterious import that all his customer's mathematical proficiency was unable to make out what it was all about. First he set down a long row of figures, which he added together with much difficulty, and then seemed to instantly conceive the most unrelenting hostility to the sum total. The mathematical tortures to which he put that unhappy amount; the arithmetical abuse which he heaped upon it, and the algebraic contumely with which he overwhelmed it, almost defy description. He first belabored it with the four simple rules; he stretched it with Addition; he cut it in two with Subtraction; he made it top-heavy with Multiplication, and tore it to pieces with Division—then he extracted its square root; then extracted the cube root of that, which left nothing of the unfortunate sum total but a small fraction, which he then divided by *ab*, and made "equal to" an infinitesimal part of some unknown *x*. Having thus wreaked his vengeance on the unhappy number, he laid away the surviving fraction in a cold corner of the slate, where he left it, first, however, giving a parting token of his bitter malignity by writing the minus sign before it, which made it perpetually worse than nothing, and reduced it to a state of irredeemable algebraic bankruptcy. This praiseworthy object being finally achieved, he proceeded to translate into intelligible English the result of his calculations, which he announced in the terms following:

"The testimonial is not the most sanguine. If the time of birth is given correct there is reason to apprehend that something of an affective nature occurred at about eight years and ten months—at

16 × 10 I think I may say, if the time of birth is given correct, there is from the figures reason to expect that there is a probability of a similar sitiwation of events. At 24 there was a favorable sitiwation of events, if there was not somebody or somethin' afflictive on the contrary, the which I am disposed to think might be possible. At 25, if the time of birth is given correct, there is reason to expect great likelihoods of some success in life; I may, it is true, be mistaken in my calculations, but as the significators are angular, I think there is indications that such will be the sitiwation of events. At 30, if the time of birth is given correct, I think you are an individdyal as may look for some species of misfortin—there will be some rather singular circumstances occur, which might denote loss of friends, or the fallin' to you of a fortin, or great travellin' by water or land, or losin' money at cards, or breakin' your leg, or makin' a great discovery, or inventin' somethin', or gettin' put into prison on suspicion of sorcery and witchcraft. You will see that there are indications to denote that you will certainly be accused of sorcery and witchcraft by some individdyals who are not your friends—the indications denote great likelihoods that this will make you uneasy in your mind, but I think there is nothin' of a very serious natur' to be feared at that time of life, if the time of birth is given correct. When any misfortin' is comin' upon you there is no doubt (though I am not goin' to state positively that such will be the case, still there is strong likelihoods that the indications give such a probability) that it will give you warnin' of its approach. At 36, if the time of birth

is given correct, there is indications of a likelihood that you will fall upon some other misfortin'; I am not prepared to state positively that such will be the case, but I think you will have a misfortin', though I don't think it would be of a very afflictive natur'. There is at that time a circumstance of an unfriendly natur', though it may not happen to yourself; it might denote that your brother will get sick. There is another evil condition about this time which I will examine still furder. I see that there is indications of a likelihood that there is a probability of your having somethin' amiss by a partner, if somethin' of a favorable natur' does not interpose, which is not unlikely, though I may be mistaken and will not say positively. You will be lucky, however, after that, and many of your evils will gradually begin to recline, as it were. There is reason to believe that the significators denote that in the course of your futur' life you will sometimes be thrown in with men who you will think is your friends, but who will prove to be your enemy. This I will not say positively, for I may be mistaken, which I think I am not, but if the time of birth is correct, you are an individdyal as gives likelihoods that such might be the case."

For more than an hour had the Inquirer been edified and instructed by these "solid chunks of wisdom," which, it will be remembered, were not delivered off-hand, but were carefully ciphered out by elaborate calculations on the slate aforesaid. Lucid and elegant as was the language, and interesting as was the matter of these oracular communications, he felt it to be his duty to interrupt them for a time and change the subject to a theme in which he felt a nearer interest; accordingly he asked the musty Seer about his prospects of future wedded bliss. This was a subject of so great importance that all the other calculations had to be erased from the slate—this little operation was accomplished in the manner of the schoolboys who haint got any sponge, and the dirty hand plied briskly for a minute between the juicy mouth and the dingy slate, and became a shade grimier by this cleanly process. Then a new horoscope was drawn with more signs of the zodiac than ever, and in due time the result was thus announced:

"I shall now endeavor to give you a description of the sort of person you might be most likeliest to marry. There is indications that your wife might be respectable. The significators do not denote that there is a likelihood that you might marry a very old woman. She would be as likely to have fair hair and blue eyes as anything else; nor would she be likely to be very much too tall, and I don't imagine you are an individdyal that might be likely to marry a woman who was very short. She may not be very old, but I do not think that the indications point her out as being likely to be a child; in fact, I think it possible that she may be of the ordinary age, though I do not wish to be understood as being positive on all these points, for I may be mistaken, though I think you will find that there is a likelihood that these things may be so. You will be married twice, and I think you are an individdyal that would be likely to have children—six children I think there is indications that you may be likely to have. The significators point out one very evil condition, and I think I may say that I'm quite sure. I'm positive that you will separate from your first wife. No, I will not say that yours is a quarrelsome natur', but the significators look bad. Things is worse, in fact, than I told you of, and now I look again and am sure you are prepared, I will say that there cannot be a doubt that *you will pizon your first wife*. It cannot be any other way; there is no mistake; it is so; it must be true; the fact is this, and thus I tell you, *you will pizon your first wife*. And, my young friend, I will advise you, in case your married futur' is unhappy, and you do find it necessary to give pizon to your consort, do not tell anybody of your intentions; do not let it be known; and you must do it in such a way as not to be suspected, or people will think hard of you, and there may be trouble."

This was a touch of wisdom for which Johannes was not prepared; so he snatched his hat and hastily left the sepulchral premises, conscious of his inability to receive another such a "chunk" without being completely floored.

He now expresses the opinion that Dr. Wilson wanted to get the job of "pizoning" that first wife, and that he would have done it with pleasure at less than the market price.

CHAPTER VIII.

Gives a history of how Mrs. Hayes, the Clairvoyant, of No. 176 Grand Street, does the Conjuring Trick.

CHAPTER VIII.

MRS. HAYES, A CLAIRVOYANT, No. 176 GRAND STREET.

There are a dozen or more of these "Clairvoyants" in the city who profess to cure diseases, and to work other wonders by the aid of their so-called wonderful power. As their mode of proceeding is very much the same in all cases, a description of one or two will give an idea of the whole. Their principal business is to prescribe for bodily ills, and did they confine themselves to this alone, they would not be legitimate subjects of mention in this book. But in addition to their medical practice they also tell about "absent friends;" tell whether projected business undertakings will fall out well or ill; whether contemplated marriages will be prosperous or otherwise: whether a person will be "lucky" in life, whether his children will be happy, and, in short, they do pretty much the regular fortune-telling routine, whenever the questions of the customer lead that way.

The theory as given by them, of a Clairvoyant diagnosis of a malady, is this: that the Clairvoyant, when thrown by mesmeric influence into the "trance" state, is enabled to *see into the body of the patient* and discern what organs, if any, are deranged, and in what manner; or to ascertain precisely the nature of the morbific condition of the body, and having thus discovered what part of the vital mechanism is out of order, they are able, they argue, to prescribe the best means for restoring the apparatus to a normal state.

There are many thousands of persons who believe this stuff, and endanger their lives and health by trusting to these empirics. Several of the most popular of them have as many patients as they can attend to, and are rapidly amassing fortunes. Most of them have a superficial knowledge of Medicine, and are thus enabled to do, with a certain amount of impunity, many dark deeds. It is reported of more than one of these women that she has done as many deeds of child-murder as did even the notorious Madame Restell.

In this regard, they are among the most dangerous and criminal of all the Witches.

The "Individual" visited Mrs. Hayes, who is one of the most ignorant of the whole lot, and Mrs. Seymour, who is one of the most intelligent of all. He sets down the particulars of his visit to the former, in the words following:

How the "Individual" sees a Clairvoyant—How he pays a Dollar, and what he gets for his money.

Not all the sorcery of all the sorcerers; not all the necromancy of all the necromancers; not all the conjurations of all masculine conjurers; not all the magic of all male magicians; not all the charming of all the charmers, charm they never so wisely, could have induced Johannes to ever more place the slightest trust in a wizard, or repose in any wonderworker of the bearded sex the merest trifle of faith, even the most infinitesimal trituration of the homœopathicest grain. The single dose he had received from the renowned Doctor Wilson was quite enough, and had satisfied all his longings for wisdom of that sort.

Besides, his coming events cast such peculiar and very unpleasant shadows before, that he preferred to keep out of the grim presence of such shady men, and for all after time to bask him only in the sunshine of smiling women.

"*Pizon his first wife*," would he? Well, he could have taken that "pizon" with tolerable composure from the lips of lovely woman, but to receive it from the mumbling mouth of a skinny old man, was too much to accept without divers rebellious grins.

A peach-cheeked witch, a cherry-lipped conjuress; a Circe, with only enough charms to make a respectable photograph, might with impunity have called him a counterfeiter, or a horse-thief, or even a thimble-rigger; or might have told him that he would, upon opportunity, garotte his grandmother for the small price of seventy cents and her snuff-box; or that he was in the habit of attending funerals to pick the pockets of the mourners, and of going to church that he might steal the pennies from the poor-box, all this would he have borne uncomplainingly from a woman; but these unpalatable statements from one of the masculine gender would be "most tolerable and not to be endured."

He felt that if he had not rushed incontinently from the presence of that underground star-gazer Dr. Wilson, he must either have punched that respected person's venerated head, or have laughed in his honored face. In either case he would, of course, have roused the extensive ire of that potent worthy, and have been at once exposed to a fire of supernatural influences that would have been probably unpleasant, to say the least.

The unmusical Johannes looks upon accordeons as cruel instruments of refined torture, and detests them as the vilest of all created or invented things, and he had been very careful to offend none of the magic community, lest he should, by some high-pressure power of their enchanted spells, be transformed into an accordeon, and be condemned to eternally have shrieking music pulled out of his bowels by unrelenting boys.

Having this terrible possible doom continually before his mind's optics, he felt that it would be only the part of prudence to avoid the company of those black art professors in whose presence he could not keep all his feelings well in hand. So, no more wizards would he visit, but the witches should henceforth have his entire attention.

It is a fortunate circumstance that there are no other men than the aforesaid Doctor Wilson, in the witch business in New York, so that there would be no temptation to break this resolve, and he probably would not be troubled to keep it.

There is one breed of the modern witch that pretends to a sort of superiority in blood and manners, and those who practise this peculiar branch of the business put on certain aristocratic airs and utterly refuse to consort with those of another stamp. They disdain the title of "Astrologers," or "Astrologists," as most of them phrase it, and in their advertisements utterly repudiate the idea that they are "Fortune Tellers."

These are the "Clairvoyants," who do business by means of certain select mummeries of their own, and who make a great deal of money in their trade. There are a great number of these in the city, so many indeed that the business is over-done, and the price of retail clairvoyance has come materially down. The same dose of this article that formerly cost five dollars, may now be had for fifty cents, and the quality is not deteriorated, but is quite as good now as it ever was.

To one of these supernatural women did the hero resolve to pay his next visit, and he selected the abode of Mrs. Hayes, of 176 Grand Street, for his initiatory consultation.

With the mysterious psychological phenomena denominated by those who profess to know them best, "clairvoyant manifestations," Johannes had nothing to do, and was content, as every one of the uninitiated must perforce be, to accept the say-so of the spiritualistic journals that there are such phenomena and that they are unexplained and mysterious. No outside unbelievers in Spiritualism and the kindred arts may ever know anything of clairvoyant developments and demonstrations, save such one-sided varnished statements as the journals that deal in that sort of commodities choose to lay before the world. Every man must be spiritually wound up to concert pitch before he is in a condition to receive the highest revelations of the clairvoyant speculators. So that, whether the clairvoyance that is sold for money be a spurious or a superfine article few can tell. Certain it is that it is the same sort of stuff that has ever been retailed to the public under the name of clairvoyance, ever since the discovery of that remunerative humbug. It is more than likely that the twaddle of Mrs. Hayes, Mrs. Seymour, and the rest of the fortune-telling crew, would be repudiated by Andrew Jackson Davis and the rest of the spiritualistic firstchoppers, but it is none the less true that these gifted women sell their pretended knowledge of spirits and spiritual persons and things, with as much pretentiousness to unerring truth, as that veritable seer himself, and at a much lower price.

The clairvoyant department of modern witchcraft is necessarily carried on by a partnership, and one which is not identical with the legendary league with the devil. Two visible persons constitute the firm, for it takes a double team to do the work, and if the amiable gentleman just referred to makes a third in the concern, he is a silent partner who merely furnishes capital, while his name is not known in the business. The whole theory of clairvoyance as applied to fortune-telling and other branches of cheap necromancy, seems to be somewhat like this.

A strong-minded person, generally a man with a *physique* like a Centre-Market butcher boy, obtains by some means possession of an extra soul or two, or spirit, or whatever else that intangible thing may be called. These spirits are always second-rate articles, not good enough to be put into vigorous and strong bodies, and which have been therefore hastily cased up in an inferior kind of human frame as a sort of make-shift for men and women.

Your professional clairvoyant is always, both as to soul and body, a botched-up job that nature ought to be ashamed of, and probably is, if she'd own up.

The senior partner of the clairvoyant fortune-telling firm, the strong-minded one, according to their professions, has the arbitrary control of the cast-off souls that animate these refuse bodies. By what spiritual hocus-pocus this is managed is not known to those outside the trade. He uses their half-baked spirits at his will, and makes his living by farming them out to do dirty jobs for the paying public. He disconnects them from their mortal vehicles, and sends them on errands in the spirit-land in behalf of his customers, looking up their "absent friends," both in and out of the body—telling of their health and prosperity if they are still alive, and picking up little bits of scandal about their angels if they are dead. The senior partner also sends his abject two-and-sixpenny souls to explore the bodies of his sick customers and examine their internal machinery, point out any little defects or disarrangements, and suggest the proper remedies therefor, and in short, to do whatever other dirty work the customer may choose to pay for.

The senior partner of course pockets all the money, merely keeping the mortal tenement in which the working partner dwells in a good state of repair, in consideration of services rendered.

Such a partnership is the one of Mr. and Mrs. Hayes, whose place of business is advertised every day in the morning papers in the words following:

"Clairvoyance.—Astonishing cures and great discoveries daily made by Mrs. Hayes, that superior and wonderful clairvoyant. All diseases discovered and cured (if curable). Unerring advice given respecting persons in business, absent friends, &c. Satisfactory examinations given in all cases, or no charge made. Residence, 176 Grand St. N. Y."

Johannes, whose general health was excellent, and whose internal apparatus was all right so far as heard from, had therefore no occasion to be astonishingly cured, or to have any great discoveries made in him by Mrs. Hayes; still he was desirous of a little "unerring advice about absent friends," etc., from "that superior and wonderful clairvoyant."

Besides, it was barely possible that in the person of the superior and wonderful Mrs. Hayes, he might find the bride for whom he pined. With hope slightly renewed within his speculative breast, he set off joyfully for the designated domicile, which he achieved in the due course of travel.

The house No. 176 Grand Street is a brick two-story dwelling, of a dingy drab color, as though it had been steeped in a Quaker atmosphere and had there imbibed its color, which had since been overlaid with "world's people's" dirt.

The door was opened by Mrs. Hayes in person, her body on this occasion being sent with her spirit to do a bit of drudgery.

She is a woman of the most abject and cringing manner imaginable; a female counterpart of Uriah Heep, with an unknown multiplication of that vermicular gentleman's writhings; she wore no hoops, she would have squirmed herself out of them in an instant; her dress was fastened securely on with numerous visible hooks and eyes, and pins, and strings, in spite of which precautions her visitor expected to see her worm out of it before she got up stairs, and would scarcely have been astonished to see her jerk her skeleton out of her skin, and complete her errand in her bones.

With a propitiating bow, whose intense servility would have become Mr. Sampson Brass in the day of his discomfiture, she asked her customer into the house, cringingly preceded him up stairs, deferentially placed a chair, and abjectly departed into an inner room, pausing at the door to execute an obsequious wriggle, and to once more humble herself in the dust (of which there was plenty) before her astonished visitor.

The reception-room to which she led him, is an apartment of moderate size, from the front windows of which the beholder may regale his eyes with a comprehensive view of Centre Market and its charming surroundings; Mott and Mulberry Streets lie just beyond, and the Tombs are visible in the dim distance.

The room was furnished with a superfluity of gaudy furniture; and sofas, tables, chairs and pictures, crowded and elbowed each other, showing plainly that the upholstery of a couple, at least, of parlors had been there compressed into a bedroom.

From the inner room came a great sound, made up of so many household ingredients as to defy accurate analysis—but the crying of babies, the frizzling of cooking meat, the scraping of saucepans, and a sound of somebody scolding everybody else, predominated.

The voyager was unprepared for any *Mister* Hayes, having taken it for granted that the *Mrs.* of the superior and wonderful clairvoyant did not imply a husband, but was merely assumed because it looks more dignified in the advertisement. But there *was* a *Mr.* Hayes, and presently the door opened and that worthy appeared; he was surrounded by an atmosphere of fried onions, and the fragrant and greasy perspiration in his face seemed to have been distilled from that favorite vegetable.

Mr. Hayes is a tall, fierce, sharp-spoken man, of manners so very rough and bearish that his wife and children quailed when he spoke as if they expected an instant blow. We don't know that it ever will be possible for a man to garrote his guardian angel for the sake of her golden crown, but the idea occurred to Johannes that if that amiable feat is ever accomplished, it will be by such another man as this. He seemed as unable to speak a kind or gentle word as to pull his boots off over his ears. He is an Englishman, and speaks with the most intolerable cockney accent. Moderating his harsh tones until they were almost as pleasant as the threatenings of an ill-natured bull-dog, and addressing his auditor, he growled out the following specimen of delectable English:

"There is lots of folks goin' round town pretendin' to do clairvoyance, and to cure sick folks, and to tell fortunes, and business, and journeys, and stole property; but we ain't none of them people. We only do this for the sake of doin' good, and we don't want to do nothin' that will make any trouble. We used to tell things about stole property, and about family troubles, and so we sometimes used to get folks into musses, but we don't do nothin' of that kind now. If your business is about any kind of muss and trouble in your family we don't want nothin' to do with it. Sometimes folks that has quarrelled their wives away come to us and wants us to get them back again, but we don't do nothing of that sort. We can tell 'em if their wives are well, or if they're sick and all about what ails 'em, and so we can about any people that is gone off anywhere, and them's what we call 'absent friends.' So if you've got any trouble with your wife we can't do nothin' for you."

The love-lorn visitor had no wives, a fact known to the reader already, and when he does accumulate a help-meet, he sincerely trusts she may not be so unruly as to require the interference of outsiders to preserve harmony in the family. He expressed himself to that effect, and added that his business was to find out about the well-being of some friends in Minnesota, and to ascertain particulars about some other trifles necessary to his peace of mind.

Hereupon Mr. Hayes, with a growl like a sulky rhinoceros, opened the door which cut off the pot-and-kettle Babel of the other room, and commanded his wife to come, and that estimable lady, who is evidently in a state of excellent subordination, instantly writhed herself into the room. She sat down in an armchair, and began to evolve a most remarkable series of inane smiles, each one of which began somewhere down her throat, rose to her mouth by jerks, and finally faded away at the top of her head and the tips of her ears. It was a purely spasmodic thing of disagreeable habit, without a particle of geniality or feeling about it.

While this curious process was going on, the Doctor had drawn down the window-shades, thus darkening the room, and now approached for the purpose of unhooking from its earthly tabernacle the soul that was to step up to Minnesota and bring back word to his customer "how all the folks got along." This he accomplished by a few mysterious mesmeric passes, and when the trance was induced, and the spirit had, so to speak, tucked its breeches into its boots ready for the muddy journey, he placed in the hand of Johannes that of the corpus which still remained in the armchair, and said to the disembodied spirit:

"Now, I want you to go with this gentleman to Brooklyn and take a fair start from there, and then go where he tells you to, and tell him what things there is there that you see."

Having delivered this injunction in a tone so indescribably savage that he had better a thousand times have struck her in the face, this amiable animal retired to the Babel, taking with him the fried-onion atmosphere.

Then the woman in the chair began to speak, in a style the most disagreeable and affected that anybody ever listened to. It was more like that sickening gibberish that nurses call "*baby-talk*," than anything else in the world. She spoke with a detestable whine, and pronounced each syllable of every word separately, as if she feared a two-syllable word might choke her. Sick at the stomach as was her visitor at the whole babyish performance, he so far controlled his qualms as to note down the words hereunder written.

Whoever has heard this woman in a professional way can testify to the verbatim truth of this sketch.

"There is wa-ter that we must cross, we must go in a boat musn't we? Now we're in the boat, and O I see so many put-ty things, men, and dogs, and ships and things going up and down; such beau-ti-ful things I have never seened before. Now we are a-cross the riv-er, and now we must get on the car, musn't we? What car must we get on? O I see it now, the yellow car. Now we are going a-long and I can see—O what a pret-ty dress in that store. O what real nice can-dy that is. I wish I had some don't you? Now we're at the house. Is it the one on the cor-ner, or the next one to it, or is it the brick house with the green blinds? No, the wood one with green blinds; so it is, but I didn't be here be-fore ev-er in my life. Now we will go in-to the house; I see a car-pet there and some chairs and some—O what a pret-ty pic-ture, and what a nice fire. I see a la-dy of ver-y pret-ty ap-pear-ance. She is a young la-dy; she has got blue eyes, she is stand-ing sideways so I can't see noth-ing of her but one side of her face. There is al-so an el-der-ly la-dy, but I can't see much of her. They appear to be go-ing on a jour-ney, shall I go with them? Yes, well I will. Now we are on the wa-ter and—O what a pret-ty boat—now we are get-ting off of the boat—I didn't nev-er be here be-fore. Now we are on a rail-road, I nev-er seened this rail-road be-fore but—O what a pret-ty ba-by. Now we go along, along, along, along, and now we are at the de-pot. I didn't ev-er be here ei-ther—there is a riv-er here, and a mill and a—O what a pret-ty cow—somebody is go-ing to milk the cow. There is a town here—it seems as if I did be here before—yes I am sure—O what a pret-ty lit-tle car-riage, and what a pret-ty dog. Yes I am sure I seened this town be-fore, but these rail-roads didn't be here then."

By this time the travellers were supposed to have reached St. Paul, and the reliable clairvoyant then proceeded to describe that interesting young city; and in the course of her speech made more improvements there than will be accomplished in reality in less than a year or two certainly.

Among other things, Mrs. Hayes described as at present existing in St. Paul, two Colleges, a City Hall built of white marble, a locomotive factory, and a place where they were building seven ocean steamers.

She then, when she arrived at the house, in the course of her mesmeric journey, where the people concerning whom Johannes had inquired were supposed to be at that present domiciled, proceeded to give descriptions of those whom she saw there, of the looks of the country and of the house.

And *such* descriptions, as much like the truth as a ton of "T" rail is like a boiled custard.

By asking leading questions the seeker after clairvoyant knowledge got some very original information. He only began this course after he found that she, if left to herself, could describe nothing, and could utter no speech more coherent or sensible than that already set down as coming from her illustrious lips.

In fact, the policy of the clairvoyant-witch in every case, is to wait for leading questions from the anxious inquirer, so that the answers may be framed to suit the exigencies of the case. Johannes was not slow to perceive this, and by way of testing the science, or rather, art of clairvoyance, he put a series of questions which established the following interesting facts, all of which were positively averred to be true by Mrs. Hayes, "that superior and wonderful clairvoyant."

Minnesota Territory is a small town situated 911 miles south-east of the mouth of the Mississippi River—its officers are a chief cook and 23 high privates, besides the younger brother of Shakspeare, who is the Mayor of the Territory, and whose principal business it is to keep the American flag at half-mast, upside down.

When this last important information had been elicited, Johannes, who thought he had got the worth of his money, recalled Dr. Hayes, who reappeared, surrounded by the same old atmosphere of the same old onions; to him the customer resigned the hand of the twaddling adult baby who had held his hand for an hour and a half, paid his dollar, and then prepared to depart.

The soul of the woman then returned from its long journey, and was locked up in its squirmy body by the Doctor, ready to serve future customers at one dollar a head.

She didn't seem glad to get her soul back again, there probably not being enough to give her any great joy, after she had got it.

Johannes turned moodily away, feeling that the conjuress, his future bride, the renovator of his broken fortunes, and the ready relief to his present necessities, was as far distant as ever.

CHAPTER IX.

Tells all about Mrs. Seymour, the Clairvoyant, of No. 110 Spring Street, and what she had to say.

CHAPTER IX.

MRS. SEYMOUR, CLAIRVOYANT, No. 110 SPRING STREET.

This woman is at the same time one of the most pretentious and most clever of the clairvoyants, and she does a very large business. Most of her customers come for medical advice, although, in accordance with her printed announcement, she is willing to talk about "absent friends," and whatever other business the client may choose to pay for.

One branch of the clairvoyant trade which formerly brought as much money to their pockets as any other department of their business, was the finding lost or stolen property, and giving directions for the detection of the thieves. This specialty has however been pretty much abandoned of late by nearly all of them, in consequence of law-proceedings against certain ones of the sisterhood, which have in three or four instances been commenced by parties who have been wrongfully accused of theft, through the agency of the clairvoyant impostors. Several suits have been instituted against them for defamation of character, and they have been made to smart so severely that they are now all very careful about accusing persons of crimes.

As an evidence of the implicit faith put in these people by their dupes, it may be mentioned that many applications have been made to Judge Welsh, of this city, and to the other judges, for warrants of arrest against respectable persons, for theft, the only grounds of suspicion against them being, that some clairvoyant had said that the property had been stolen by a person of such and such a height, with hair and eyes of this or that color, and that the suspected person happened to answer the description. Of course, all such applications for legal process have been refused by the magistrates, and the applicants dismissed with a severe rebuke.

Mrs. Seymour was an intimate friend of Mrs. Cunningham, of the Burdell-murder notoriety, and was a witness in that memorable trial.

The Cash Customer had an interview with this woman, which he thus describes:

Another Clairvoyant, who is not much in particular.

If a man be desirous of knowing what sort of a moral character he bears in the spirit-world, and what style of society his disembodied soul will circulate in, or if he desires to know the particulars of the after-death behavior of any of his acquaintances, of course he will find it to his interest to marry a "medium" of average respectability, and in good practice, and so save the expense of frequent consultations. The "rapping" and "table-tipping" communications from the spirit-world are hardly satisfactory. It is, very likely, pleasant for a man to be on speaking terms with his bedroom furniture, to spend an agreeable hour occasionally in conversation with his washhand-stand, to enjoy a spirited argument with his bedstead and rocking-chair, or to receive now and then a confidential communication from his bootjack, but on the whole, these upholstery dialogues do not satisfy the "yearnings of the soul after the infinite." The powers of speech of a washhand-stand are circumscribed, bedsteads and rocking-chairs are seldom equal to a sustained conversation, and the most talkative bootjack has not a sufficient command of language to make itself agreeable for any great length of time. The logic of a poker may sometimes be convincing, but it is not generally agreeable; and the rhetoric of uneducated coal-scuttles is hardly elegant enough to pass the criticism of a refined taste. It is therefore much more satisfactory as well as economical, for a person who desires to enjoy his daily chat with the Spirits, to get a "speaking medium" to translate the eloquence of all parties and make the thing pleasant. Even then, confidential communications must be very guarded, and on this account the person who invents some means by which every man can be his own medium, will win an equal immortality with the author of that invaluable book, "Every Man his own Washerwoman."

Johannes had been thinking over the spiritual subject, of course with a view to profitable matrimony, for he thought he could manage to turn an intimacy with the spirits to good pecuniary account, and inveigle those incorporeal gentlemen into doing something for those of their friends who are yet bothered with bodies.

He knew that there are in New York, plenty of spiritualists in such constant communication with their acquaintances on the "other side of Jordan," that they know the bill of fare with which those seventh-heaveners are served every day, and whenever their jolly ghostships sit down to a pleasant game of whist, they send word to their earthly relatives by "medium" every fresh deal, what the new trump is, who hold the honors, and how the game stands generally.

So close a familiarity with superior beings as this, could be easily turned to practical account and made to pay handsomely, by a Spiritualist with a utilitarian turn of mind. If he could but get his spirits into proper subjection how useful would they not be in the patent medicine business, in the way of inventing new remedies; how invaluable would they be to an editor; in fact, how particularly useful in almost any kind of business.

But his great plan was to train a corps of light-footed and gentle ghosts to carry news; they would of course beat locomotives, carrier pigeons, and electric telegraphs out of sight; seas, mountains, and such trifling obstacles would be no hindrance to them, and the Associated Press, to say nothing of the Board of Brokers, would pay handsomely for their services. Of course a ghost with any pretensions to speed would bring us detailed news from London in half-an-hour or so, without putting himself out of breath in the least, thus beating the telegraph by a length. And so Johannes, fully determined on this promising scheme, began to cast about him for a medium who was acquainted in the spirit sphere, to introduce him to some of the eligible ghosts.

He knew that most of the clairvoyant women are "mediums," and thought very naturally that women who already earned their living by clairvoyance, would be the very ones to enter heart and soul with him into his spiritualistic scheme.

Yes, he would marry a medium, and if she was a professional clairvoyant, so much the better, his bow would have another string.

In his search for a witch-wife he would not have been justified in interfering at all with the clairvoyants had it not been for the fact that they mix a little witchcraft with their regular business. Their ostensible trade is to diagnose and prescribe for different varieties of internal disease, and so this particular branch of humbug would not have come within the scope of the voyager's investigations, were it not that several of these practitioners advertise to "tell the past, present, and future, describe the future husband or wife, mark out correctly the exact course of future life, give unerring advice about business, absent friends, etc."

All this had too strong a savor of witchcraft to be ignored, and accordingly Johannes set forth on his journey to visit another of these mysteriously clear-sighted persons, keeping in view all the time the probabilities of her being an A I spiritual medium, and the very person whose aid would be invaluable in his new journalistic enterprise.

Mrs. Seymour, of No. 110 Spring Street, was the person towards whose house the Cash Customer bent his steps, after reading the subjoined advertisement of her powers and capabilities.

"Clairvoyance.—Mrs. Seymour, 110 Spring Street, a few doors west of Broadway, the most successful medical and business Clairvoyant in America. All diseases discovered and cured, if curable; unerring advice on business, absent friends, &c., and satisfaction in all cases, or no charge made."

The clairvoyant branch of the fortune-telling business seems to require a certain amount of respectability in its practices, and they sneer at the grosser deceptions of the more vulgar of the necromantic trade. They keep aloof from the greasier sisters of the profession, and they feel it due to the dignity of their station to reject the cards, the magic mirrors, the Bibles and keys, the mysterious pebbles and the other tricks which do well enough for twenty-five cent customers; to sojourn in reputable streets, in respectable houses, and to have clean faces when visitors come in. There are, it is true, clairvoyants in the city who live wretchedly in miserable cellars, whose garments and very hair are populated with various specimens of animated nature, and whose bodies are so filthy that the beholder wonders why the spirits, which are so often disconnected from them and sent on far-off missions, do not avail themselves of the leave of absence to desert for ever such unsavory corporeal habitations. But the majority of these persons prefer parlors to basements, and make up the difference in expenses by double-charging their customers. Many of them, as before stated, combine a little spiritualism of the other sort with the clairvoyance, and they can all go into a trance on short notice and rhapsodize with all the fervor if not the eloquence of Mrs. Cora Hatch; they can all do the table-tipping trick, and are up to more rappings than the Rochester Fox girls ever thought of. For these several reasons therefore Mrs. Seymour would be a wife worth having, or at least so thought Johannes as he pondered these truths, and arranged in his mind his plan of attack on the affections of that susceptible lady.

The house No. 110 Spring Street, occupied by Mrs. Seymour for business purposes, is not more seedy in appearance than the majority of half-way decent tenant houses, which all have a decrepit look after they are four or five years old, as though youthful dissipations had made them weak in the joints. From appearances, Mrs. Seymour's house had been more than commonly rakish in its juvenility, but it still had that look of better days departed, which, in the human kind, is peculiar to decayed ministers of the gospel. It is a house where a man on a small salary would apply for cheap board. Hither the inquirer repaired, and shamefacedly knocked at the door, and was admitted by a frowzy, coarse, plump, semi-respectable girl, who would have been the better for a washing. She opened the door and the customer entered the reception-room, and had ample time before the appearance of the mistress to take an observation.

The parlor was neatly, though rather scantily furnished, with a rigid economy in the article of chairs.

The apartment communicated by folding-doors with another room, whence could be heard an iron noise as of some one scraping a saucepan with a kitchen-spoon. The frowzy girl disappeared into this retired spot, and in about the space of time that would be occupied by an enterprising woman in rolling down her sleeves, taking off her apron, and washing her hands, the door opened, and Mrs. Seymour presented herself.

She was a frigid-looking woman, of about 35 years of age, with dark hair and eyes, projecting lips and heavy chin, and was of medium height and size. Her appearance was perhaps lady-like, her movements slow and well considered. She was perfectly self-possessed and calculating, and appeared to cherish no dissatisfaction with herself. Her demeanor, on the whole, was repelling and chilly, and impressed her visitor very much as if some one had slipped a lump of ice down his back and made him sit on it till it melted.

She regarded him with a look of professional suspicion, cast her eye round the room with a quick glance, which instantly inventoried everything therein contained, as though to assure herself of the safety of any small articles which might be scattered about, and then seated herself with an air of preparedness, as if she was perfectly on guard and not to be taken by surprise by anything that might occur. She volunteered a frozen remark or two about the state of the weather, and then subsided into silence, evidently waiting to hear the object of the visit.

Her appearance and demeanor had instantly frozen out of the voyager's mind all thoughts of marriage; he would as soon have wedded an iceberg, or have taken to his heart of hearts a thermometer with its mercury frozen solid. All he could do was to buy a dollar's worth of her clairvoyance and then get out.

As soon therefore as the first chill had passed off, and he had thawed out a few words for immediate use he asked for a little of that commodity.

When as he announced that he desired to know about the present well or ill of some absent friends, and that clairvoyance was the branch of her business which would on this occasion be called into requisition, she rose from her seat, walked to the door, never taking her eyes from the hands and pockets of her customer, and called to some one to come in. In obedience to the summons, the frowzy girl entered; this latter individual, since her first appearance, had taken off her apron and pinned some kind of a collar around her neck, but had not yet found time to comb her hair, which was exceedingly demonstrative, and forced itself upon attention.

Mrs. Seymour seated herself in a rocking-chair and closed her eyes; the plump girl stood behind her and pressed her thumbs firmly upon the temples of Mrs. S. for about two minutes, during which time this latter lady lost every instant something of life and animation, until at last she froze up entirely. Then the frowzy girl made one or two mysterious mesmeric passes over the sleeping beauty from her head to her feet, to fix her in the iceberg state; then placing the hand of Mrs. S. in the palm of the customer, she left the room.

The worst of it was that Mrs. Seymour's hand is not an agreeable one to hold; it is cold and flabby, and not suggestive of vitality. Her face, too, had become pallid and corpse-like, and her thin blue lips were not pleasant to regard. Johannes was puzzled; he didn't know what to do with the flabby hand, and how he was to get any information about absent friends from a fast-asleep woman he did not, as yet, exactly comprehend. At this juncture, the lips asked, "Where am I to go to?" The sitter suppressed a sulphurous reply, and substituted, "To Minnesota." Thereupon, without any more definite direction as to what part of that rather extensive territory she was expected to visit, she sent her spirit off, and immediately uttered these words:

"I see two old people, two *very* old people—one is a man and one is a woman; one of them has been very sick of bilious fever, but is now better, and will soon be quite well again. I can't tell exactly how these people look except that they are very old and both are very grey. They may be husband and wife. I think they are. They are both sitting down now. I also see two young people—one of them is a male and the other a female. The male I do not perceive very plainly, and I cannot make out much about him; he seems to be standing up and looking very sad, but I can't tell you a great deal about him. The female I can see much better, and can make out more about. She is tall, and has dark hair. She appears to be connected in some way to the old people, but I do not think she is related to the young man, though I cannot exactly make out. She is a very agreeable-looking female, rather pretty, I should say, if not positively handsome. She has straight hair and does not wear curls. She is standing up now, and appears to be talking to the young man, who has his back partly turned toward her. I don't quite make out what they are saying. She has had a very severe attack of sickness, but has nearly or quite recovered. She is not, however, what I should call a healthy female, and she will soon have another fit of sickness, which will be worse than the first, and will bring her very low indeed—very near to death. But she will not die then, though she is not what I should call a long-lived person. She will certainly die in six or eight years. What disease she will die of I can't just make out, but it will not be of a lingering character: it will carry her off suddenly. These people are all very anxious about you, as if you was one of their family. They have not heard from you lately, and are looking daily for intelligence from you. They have written to you twice within three months. One of the letters got to this city—a man took it out of the mail. I don't know where he took it out, and I can't exactly describe the man, but a man took it out of the mail. These people are not satisfied to live where they are now; they are discontented with the country, and will return here in the Spring. They are talking about it now. They would like to come back this Winter, but circumstances are so that they cannot. You may be sure, however, that you will see them here in the Spring. There is no doubt of it; they will come here in the Spring. The other letter that I told you of that they had written has got here safe, and is now in the Post-Office. You will find it there if you inquire; you will be sure to get it as soon as you go down to the office."

This was delivered in a very jerky manner, with occasional twitchings of the face and violent claspings of the hand, which her visitor retained, although it gave him a cold sweat to do it. Johannes, who has friends in Minnesota, and whose questions were therefore all in good faith, tried to get the sleeping female to descend a little more to particulars, to describe individuals or localities minutely enough to be recognised if the descriptions approached the truth; but Mrs. Seymour was not to be caught in this manner. She invariably dodged the question, and dealt only in the most vague and uncertain generalities—giving no description of persons or things that might not have applied with equal accuracy to a hundred other persons or things in that or any other locality. Her assertions concerning the persons supposed to be her customer's friends did not approach the truth in any one particular; nor was there the slightest shadow of even probability in any single statement she uttered. She is not, however, a woman to lack customers, so long as there remain in the world fools of either sex.

When the inquirer had concluded his questioning, he was somewhat at a loss how to awake the woman from her trance, but she solved that little difficulty herself by opening her eyes (as if she had been wide awake all the time) and calling for the beauteous maiden of the snarly hair, who accordingly appeared and made a few mysterious mesmeric passes lengthwise of her sleeping mistress, and awoke her to the necessity of dunning her visitor, which she did instantly and with a relish. He paid the demanded dollar and departed.

CHAPTER X.

Describes Madame Carzo, the Brazilian Astrologist, of No.
151 Bowery, and gives all the romantic adventures of the "Individual" with that gay South American Naiad.

CHAPTER X.

MADAME CARZO, THE BRAZILIAN ASTROLOGIST, No. 151 BOWERY.

The illustrious lady who is the subject of the present chapter, came to the city of New York in 1856, and at once took lodgings and began business in the fortune-telling way. She did well, pecuniarily speaking, for a time, but the details of a visit to her having been published at length in one of the daily journals, she at once retired from the business, and subsided into private life. She is not now extant as a witch, and it is not impossible that she is earning an honester living in other ways.

The newspaper article that convinced her of the error of her ways, and induced her to give up fortune-telling, is the subjoined chapter by the "Individual: "

He meets a Yankee-Brazilian. She is not ill-looking, etc.

Whether the budding beauties of maidenhood are inconsistent with the orgies of witchcraft; whether there be an irreconcilable antagonism between youth and loveliness, and the unknown mysteries of the black art, is a vexed question of some interest. Can't a woman be supposed to indulge in a little devilment before her hair turns grey, and her teeth fall out? and is it impossible for her to have reliable and trustworthy dealings with Old Scratch until she is wrinkled and withered?

That's what I want to know.

And I am very naturally urged to the inquiry by the observation that every professional witch in New York calls herself a "Madame." There is not a "Miss" or a "Mademoiselle," in the whole batch. They all make a pretence of being widows, or wives at the very least, as if a certain amount of matrimonial tribulation was indispensable to their accomplishment in the arts of sorcery and magic. The only exception to this rule is found in the person of a female calling herself "The Gipsy Girl," who is otherwheres mentioned, and in *her* case the several agencies of nature, rum, and small-pox have made her so strikingly ugly that old age could not add a single other trait of repulsiveness to her excruciating features.

Now this is all a sad mistake. Let some young and undeniably pretty girl go into the business, and she'd soon get a run of exclusive customers who would stand any price and pay without grumbling. If the original Satan should refuse to recognise her eligibility, and should decline to furnish her with the requisite quantity of diabolic knowledge to set her up in business, she could easily find an opposition devil who would provide her stock in trade, and possibly at something less than the usual rates. I'll be bound that Lucifer doesn't monopolize the whole trade in witchcraft, and pocket all the profits himself; for if some of the numerous clerks in his employ haven't yet learned the trick of stealing the stock and selling it at a reduced price, then the young gentlemen of our earthly mercantile houses are a good deal up-to-snuffer than the virtuous demons of Mr. Satan's establishment. This last-named dealer generally demands the soul of the contracting party in return for the powers and privileges conferred; and in very many cases he must get decidedly the worst of the bargain, for some of his precious adopted children never had soul enough to pay for the ink to sign it away with; but there is no doubt, in case a brisk competition should arise for customers, that some of his cashiers and head-clerks would contrive to undersell him even at this price.

The person who is so very anxious to effect this desirable consummation, and to bring on a crop of young and pretty witches to supersede the grizzled ones of this present generation was Johannes, who had of late been getting rather sick of the "Madames," and would prefer, if possible, to have the rest of his fortunes told by ladies of tenderer age, and greater inexperience in the ways of the world.

However, he was not the man to be deterred, in his pursuit of wisdom, by the age and ugliness, grey hairs, wrinkles, false teeth, *no* teeth, dirt, ignorance, and imbecility he had encountered, and he was determined to go on to the very end and see if these are the sum total of modern witchcraft.

And then *duns* came o'er the spirit of his dream, and fond visions of sundry small debts, paid by magic and a wife, as soon as he should succeed in finding the wife who had the magic, floated across his hard-up brain, and encouraged him to perseverance in his matrimonial quest. And when he had won that invaluable lady, he would stuff his mattress with receipted bills, and cram his pillow with cancelled notes, lie down to pleasant dreams, and awake to ready cash.

Sweet thought!

So he made ready to visit the humble abode of Madame Carzo, the Brazilian Astrologist, *No. 151 Bowery.*

To say that he discovered, in this lady, the ideal of his search, that he found her handsome, intelligent, learned in the stars and thoroughly posted in the other branches of her trade, would be to anticipate. Suffice to say that boa-constrictors, half-naked savages, dyewoods, Jesuit's bark, cockatoos, scorpions and ring-tailed monkeys, are not, as he had hitherto supposed, the only contributions to the happiness of mankind afforded by South America, for the Province of Brazil grows fortune-tellers of a very superior quality as to respectability and neatness of appearance. A Brazilian witch was something new, and without stopping to inquire how she had strayed so far away from home, he immediately argued that that single fact was decidedly in her favor. Thus ran the logic:

If there be any diabolism in modern witchcraft, the practisers thereof who have received their education in tropical latitudes ought to be the most worthy of credence and belief, inasmuch as the temperature of their places of residence seems to afford a supposition that they live nearer head-quarters, and are, therefore, most likely to receive information by the shortest routes.

By the time he arrived at the spot where the great astrologist condescended to abide, he had, by this course of reasoning, convinced himself that he ought to place implicit confidence in any revelations of the future made by the mysterious woman who advertised herself and her calling, daily in the papers as follows:

"Madame Carzo, the gifted Brazilian Astrologist, tells the fate of every person who visits her with wonderful accuracy, about love, marriage, business, property, losses, things stolen, luck in lotteries, absent friends, at No. 151 Bowery, corner of Broome."

The South American lady had located her mysterious self in a fragrant spot.

The corner of Bowery and Broome Street and vicinity seems to have some kind of a constitutional disorder, and it relieves itself by a cutaneous eruption of low rum shops and pustulous beer saloons, which always look as if they ought to be squeezed and rubbed with ointment of red lead. To an observing person it appears as if the city wanted to scratch itself in that particular part to relieve the local irritation, and then ought, for the sake of its general health, to take a large dose of brimstone immediately afterward. The liquors sold at these places are those pure and healthful beverages, "warranted to kill at forty rods," and are the very drinks with which a convivial, but revengeful man, would wish to regale his friend against whom he held a secret grudge. Why Madame Carzo had chosen this particular locality, does not appear; perhaps because the liquor was cheap and the rent low. Certain it is that there she sat, at a window overlooking the Bowery, in full view of all the pedestrians in the street and the passengers in the 4th Avenue Railroad.

Madame Carzo was, doubtless, deeply attached to her old Brazilian home, and loved to surround herself with circumstances and things that would constantly and vividly recall pleasant memories of her southern country. Cherishing, probably, kindly and regretful remembrances of the harmless reptiles of her own Brazilian forests, she had taken up her abode in the very thick of the Bowery bar-rooms, as the only things afforded by our frigid climate, at all approaching in life-destroying malignity the speedier venoms to which she had been accustomed in her delightful southern home. First-rate facilities for drugging a man into a state of crazy madness are offered at the bar across the way; he may swill himself into a condition of beastly stupidity with lager beer from next door below; he may be pleasantly poisoned by degrees with the drugged alcohol, in various forms, which is sold next door above; or he may be more speedily disposed of with a couple of doses of "doctored" whiskey from the festering den just round the corner. Lucrezia Borgia was a novice, a mere babe in toxicology. New York wholesale liquor dealers could teach her the alphabet in the fine art of slow poisoning. She would no longer need the subtle chemistry of the Borgias; she could learn of them to poison wholesale and to do the work by labor-saving machinery.

Johannes, resolved that if he should marry the astrologist he would move out of the neighborhood, and take a house in a cleaner part of the city, for he felt that if he had to do even the courting here, he would have to fumigate himself after every visit to his lady-love as though he had just come out of a yellow-fever ship. He knew that if he should chance to meet the Health Officer in the street after a two hours' stay in that locality, that trusty official would, from the unhealthy smell of his coat, quarantine him for forty days, and put him up to his neck in a barrel of chloride of lime every morning.

But a full-fledged Cupid is a plucky animal, and not easily killed by anything no more tangible than smell, and the particular Cupid that had possession of the voyager's heart came of a long-suffering breed, and was equal to almost any emergency. So as Johannes did not feel his ardent passion die, or even turn sick at the stomach, he thought he could manage to get through. If he couldn't get along any other way, he could fill his pockets with brimstone matches, and his boots full of blue vitriol. Or he could carry a bunch of Chinese firecrackers in his hat, and touch them off on the sly whenever he felt himself in need of a healthy smell. Then he could wash himself all over in lime-water, and drink a quart or so of some liquid disinfectant every time he came away. So he went ahead.

Madame Carzo, the Brazilian interpreter of Yankee fate and fortunes, lives in the third story of the house No. 151 Bowery, with her sister, a girl of about fifteen years of age. The two occupy themselves with plain sewing, except when the Madame is overhauling the future and taking a look at the hereafter of some anxious inquirer, who pays her as much for the reliable information she imparts in three minutes, as she would charge him for making three shirts. The inquirer gave his customary modest ring at the door, and was admitted with as little question as if he had been the taxes, the Croton water, or the gas. Up the two flights of stairs walked the gentleman in the pursuit of witchcraft, gave a bashful knock at the door, at the side of which was painted, on a small bit of pasteboard, "Madame Carzo"—repented of his temerity before the echo of the knock had died away, but was admitted into the room before his repentance had time to develop itself into running away.

A shabby-looking girl, with her hair in as much confusion as if the city had contracted to keep it straight, with one ear-ring in her ear, and the other on the table, with her shoes down at the heel, her dress unhooked behind, and her breast-pin wrong side up, was the model young woman who had answered the knock. She had evidently been engaged in an animated single combat with another young woman, of about the same quality and age, who was seated on a low stool in the corner, for she instantly renewed hostilities by stabbing her antagonist in the arm with a needle, tapping her on the head with a thimble, and kicking her pin-cushion under the table, so she could not recover it without crawling on her hands and knees.

On a small sofa or lounge at the side of the room was a quantity of what ladies call "work," thrown down in a great hurry, with the needle yet sticking in it, and the scissors, and the beeswax, and the measuring tape, and the bodkin half-concealed inside, as if the knock at the door had startled the needle-woman, and she had flown to parts unknown. It was undoubtedly Madame Carzo herself who had so unceremoniously deserted her colors and her weapons, and Johannes looked at the needle with veneration, viewed the thimble with respect, and regarded the beeswax and the bodkin with concentrated awe.

A small cooking-stove was in the side of the room, and immediately over it was a picture of St. Andrew in such a position that he could smell all the dinners; a number of other pictures of Roman Catholic subjects were neatly framed and hanging against the wall. St. Somebody taking his ease on an X-shaped cross, St. Somebody Else comfortably cooking on a gridiron, and St. Somebody, different from either of these, impaled on a spear like a bug in an Entomological Museum. There was also an atrocious colored print labelled "Millard Fillmore," which, if it at all resembled that venerated gentleman, must have been taken when he had the measles, complicated with the mumps and toothache, and was attired in a sky-blue coat, a red cravat, yellow vest, and butternut-colored pantaloons.

The room was neatly furnished with carpet, table, chairs, cheap mirror, and a lounge. While the visitor was taking this observation, the two young ladies before mentioned had continued to spar after a feminine fashion, and had finished about three rounds; the model, who had answered the bell, had got the other one, who was black-haired and vicious, under the table, and was following up her advantage by sticking a bodkin into the tender places on her feet and ancles. When the model had at length thoroughly subjugated and subdued the black-haired one, and reduced her to a state of passive misery, she turned to her visitor with an amiable smile, and asked him if he desired to see the Madame. Receiving an affirmative reply, she gave a sly kick to her fallen foe, stepped on her toes under pretence of moving away a chair, and then disappeared into another room to inform Madame Carzo that visitors and dollars were awaiting her respectful consideration in the anteroom.

The "gifted Brazilian astrologist" regarded the suggestion with a favorable eye, for the model soon reappeared and showed the searcher after hidden knowledge into a bedroom nearly dark, wherein were several dresses hanging on the wall, a bed, two chairs, a table, and Madame Carzo. The light was so arranged as to fall directly in the face of the stranger, while the countenance of the Madame was, to a certain extent, hidden in shadow.

Johannes, nevertheless, in spite of this disadvantage, by careful observation, is enabled to give a tolerably accurate description of Madame Carzo, as follows: She is a tall, comely-looking woman, with unusually large black eyes, clear complexion, dark hair worn *à la Jenny Lind*, a small hand, clean, and with the nails trimmed, and she has a low sweet voice. Her dress was lady-like, being a neat half-mourning plaid, with a plain linen collar at the neck, turned smoothly over; altogether, Madame Carzo, the Brazilian astrologer, who speaks without a symptom of foreign accent, impressed her customer as being a transplanted Yankee school ma'am, with shrewdness enough to see that while civilization and enlightenment would only pay her twenty dollars a month, and superstition and ignorance would give her twice that sum in a week, she couldn't, of course, afford to live in a civilized and enlightened neighborhood, and depend exclusively on civilization and enlightenment for a living.

And Johannes was smitten, he had found her, and if his fortune was propitious he would yet win and wed the Brazilian astrologer, and she should have the honor of paying his debt, and earning his bread and butter. But he would make no advances yet for fear of accidents; he would not commit himself until he had called upon the rest of the witches on his list, to see, if perchance, he might not find one more eligible. If not, then by all means Madame Carzo should be the chosen one. The first thing evidently was to ascertain her proficiency in the magic arts.

The sorceress and the anxious inquirer seated themselves face to face, and the following dialogue ensued: "Do you wish to consult me, Sir?" "Yes."

"My terms are a dollar for gentlemen."

The expected dollar was handed over, when the 'cute Yankeeism of the Brazilian lady blazed out brilliantly, for she instantly produced a "Thompson's

Bank-note Detector" from under a pillow, and a one dollar note, issued by the President and Directors of the "Quinnipiack Bank" of Connecticut, underwent a severe scrutiny. At last the genuineness of the bill and the solvency of the bank were certified to the Madame's satisfaction, in his oracular pamphlet, by Thompson with a "p," and Madame Carzo was evidently satisfied that her customer didn't mean to swindle her, but was good for small debts not exceeding one dollar each. Accordingly she took his left hand, regarded it for some time, apparently delighted with its model symmetry, but at last so far conquered her silent admiration as to speak and say:

"You were born under two planets, Moon and Mars, Moon brings you a great deal of trouble in the early part of your life. Moon has occasioned a great deal of anxiety to your parents on your account. Moon made you liable to accidents and misfortunes while you was a boy, and Moon will give you great trouble until you arrive at middle age. You were born, I should say, across the water, and you will die across the water in a city, but not a great city. You are, I should say, now far away from that city, and from your home, and parents, and friends, who are, I should say, all now far across the water. You will be sure, however, I should say, for to see them all before you die, and to die in the city that I told you of. Your line of life runs to 60; you will, I should say, live to be 60, but not much after. Moon will cause you much trouble for many years, but you will be certain for to succeed well in the end, I should say. You will be certain for to have final success and to conquer every obstacle, in spite of Moon, I should say."

Incensed as was Johannes at Moon for thus unjustifiably interfering with his prospects and meddling with his private affairs, he still admired the more the profitable science of the wonderful lady whose acquirements in magic had given her so intimate an acquaintance with Moon, as to enable her to tell so exactly the plans and intentions of that unruly and adverse planet.

He mastered his indignation and listened attentively to the sequel.

On the small stand were two packs of cards of different sizes, and a volume of Byron. Madame Carzo took up one pack of the cards, presented them to the young man, waited for them to be cut three times, after which she said:

"You face up a good fortune I should say, you have had trouble but can now, I should say, see the end of it—you face up money, which is coming to you from over the water, I should say, and you will be sure for to get it before a great while. You will never have much money from relations or friends, though you will, I should say, perhaps have some—but though you will handle a great deal of money in your lifetime you will make the most of it yourself, I should say—you will not, however, I should say, ever be able for to become very rich, for you will never be able for to keep money, although you will have the handling of a great deal in your life. No, I am certain that you will never be rich."

Here Johannes remembered the malicious influence of Moon upon his fortunes, and as he clinched his fists, felt as if he would like to get at the man who resides in that ill-conditioned planet, and have a back-hold wrestle with him on stony ground.

But the astrologer continued thus: "You face up a letter; you also face up good news which is to come speedily I should say; you don't face up a sick bed, or a coffin, or a funeral, or any kind of immediate bad luck that I am able to see. You face up two men, one dark and one light complexioned. You must beware of the dark-complexioned man, for I should say he will do you an injury if you allow him for to have a chance. You like to study: the kind of business you would do best in is *doctor*. You face up a light-complexioned lady; you will, I should say, be able to marry this lady, though a dark-complexioned man stands in the way. You must, I should say, be particularly careful to beware of the dark-complexioned man. You will be married twice; your first wife will die, but your last wife, I should say, will be likely for to outlive you. You will have three children, which will be all, I should say, that you will be likely for to have."

And this was all for the present, except that she told her visitor that he might draw thirteen cards, and make a wish, which he did, and she, on carefully examining the cards, told him that he would certainly have his wish.

Cheered by this last grateful promise, and bidding a mental defiance to Moon, the traveller left the room. In the reception chamber he found the model and the black-eyed one just coming to time for what he should judge was the twenty-seventh round, both much damaged in the hair, but plucky to the last.

Johannes walked briskly away, feeling that his matrimonial prospects were brighter now than for many a day, and fully determined that if, on going further he fared worse, he would certainly retrace his steps and wed Madame Carzo off-hand.

CHAPTER XI.

In which is set down the prophecy of Madame Leander Lent, of No. 163 Mulberry Street; and how she promised her Customer numerous Wives and Children.

CHAPTER XI.

MADAME LEANDER LENT, No. 163 MULBERRY STREET.

I have before suggested, in as plain terms as the peculiar nature of the subject will allow, that these fortune-telling women, having most of them been prostitutes in their younger days, in their withered age become professional procuresses, and make a trade of the betrayal of innocence into the power of Lust and Lechery. This assertion is so eminently probable that few will be inclined to dispute it, but I wish to be understood that this is no matter of mere surmise with me—it is a proven fact. And the evidences of its truth have been gathered, not alone from the formal and hurried records of the police courts, but from the lips of certain inmates of various Magdalen Asylums who have been reclaimed from their former homes of shame; and from the mouths of other repentant women, who, under circumstances where there was no object to deceive, and at times when their hearts were full of grateful love for those who had interposed to save them from utter despair, have in all simple truthfulness and honor, related their life-histories. It is impossible to give even a plausible guess at the aggregate number of young women, in this great city, who compromise their honorable reputations in the course of a single year; but of those whose shame becomes publicly known, and especially of those who eventually enter houses of ill-repute, the percentage whose fall was accomplished through the instrumentality, more or less direct, of the professional fortune-tellers, is astounding. And a curious fact connected with this subject is, that of these unfortunates who thus wander astray, not one in ten but has ever after the most superstitious and implicit faith in the supernatural powers of the witch. Each one sees in her own case certain things that have been foretold to her by the fortune-teller with such circumstantiality of time and place, and which have afterwards "come to pass," so exactly in accordance with the prophecy, that she can only account for it by ascribing supernatural prescience to the prophetess.

The true solution of the matter is, of course, that the wonderful fulfilments are achieved by means of confederacy and collusion with parties with whom the dupe is never brought in contact; a common *modus operandi* of this sort is elsewhere described.

Nor are the fortune-tellers and the brothel-keepers by any means content with playing into each other's hands in a general sort of way; there are, in New York, several *firms*, consisting each of a fortune-teller and a mistress of a bawdy-house, who have entered into a perfectly organized business partnership, and who ply their fearful trade with as much zeal and enthusiasm as is ever exhibited in the active competition between rival commercial houses engaged in legitimate trade.

Although this fact is one that cannot be substantiated by the production of any sworn documents, it is as well proven by the observations of keen-eyed detectives attached to the police department, and to some of the charitable institutions of this city, as though attested articles of co-partnership could be exhibited with the signatures of the contracting parties attached thereto. A gentleman of this city, in whose word I have the most perfect confidence, tells me that he once, by a curious accident, overheard a business consultation between the two members of such a firm; and that such partnerships *do* exist, and that by their means hundreds of ignorant young women, of the lower classes, are every year betrayed to their moral ruin, I no more doubt than I doubt the rotundity of the earth.

If the illustrious woman who is the subject of the present chapter should ever surmise that the foregoing observations are intended to have a personal application to herself, the author will give her much more credit for sagacity and discernment than he did for supernatural wisdom.

Madame Leander Lent is one of the most shrewd, unscrupulous, and dirty of all the goodly sisterhood of New York witches. She has so great a run of customers that her doors are often besieged by anxious inquirers as early as eight o'clock in the morning, and the servant is frequently puzzled to find room and chairs to accommodate the shame-faced throng, till her ladyship sees fit to get out of bed and begin the labors of the day. She is then impartial in the distribution of her favors; the audiences are governed by barber-shop rules, and the visitors are admitted to the presence in the order of their coming, and any one going out forfeits his or her "turn" and on returning must take position at the tail end of the queue.

The Fates show no favoritism.

The quarter in which Madame Lent has domiciled herself and her familiars, is by no means in the most aristocratic part of the city. "Mulberry," is the pomological name of the street, and it has never been celebrated for its cleanliness or for its eligibility as a site for princely mansions. In fact it has been, on the whole, rather neglected by that class of society who generally indulge in palatial luxuries.

Hercules, in his capacity of an amateur scavenger, once attempted the cleaning of the Augean stables, or some such trifle, and his success was trumpeted throughout the neighborhood as a triumph of ingenuity and perseverance. If Hercules would come to Gotham and try his hand at the purgation of Mulberry Street, our word for it, he would, in less than a week, knock out his brains with his own club in utter despair.

There never yet were swine with stomachs strong enough to feed upon the garbage of its gutters, or with instincts so perverted as to wallow in its filth. Dogs, lean and wild-eyed, the outcasts of the canine world, sometimes, driven by sore stress of hunger, sneak here with drooping tails and shame-faced looks, to search for bones, and then, wounded in their self-respect by the very act, they drag their osseous provender to a distance, and upon some sunny mud-heap, dine in dainty neatness. The very pavement is broken into countless hillocks and ruts like waves, as if, in utter disgust at the place and its associations, the street was trying to roll itself away in stony billows. The shattered wrecks of worn-out drays and carts stand forsaken in the street, keeping each other dismal company, while an occasional shackly wheelbarrow makes the place look as though, after some monstrous fashion, it were a lying-in hospital for poverty-stricken vehicles, and the wheelbarrows were the new-born children, decrepit even in their babyhood. The houses in this pleasant vale have a disheartened tumble-down look, and give the impression of having been originally built by apprentices out of second-hand material. They lean maliciously over the narrow sidewalks, and keep up a constant threatening of a sudden collapse and a general smash of passers-by. If the houses are not dirtier than the street, it is only because every possible element of filth enters into the latter; if they are not dirtier inside than outside, it is because superlatives have no superlative.

Pawnbrokers' shops are plentiful, kept always by sharp-featured restless Jews, who watch for unwary passers-by like unclean beasts crouching in noisome, dangerous lairs; while bar-rooms yawn in frequent cellars to devour bodily the victims the Jews only rob.

In this, one of the dirtiest streets in this dirty metropolis, directly opposite the English Lutheran Church of St. James, in one of the dirtiest tenant-houses in the street, abideth Madame Leander Lent, the prophetess. Why the mysterious powers didn't select an earthly representative with a more reputable dwelling-place is a mystery; but there seems to be an inseparable congeniality between prophetic knowledge and concentrated nastiness, utterly beyond all power of explanation. The Madame advises the public of her business in the terms following:

"Astrology.—Madame Leander Lent can be consulted about love, marriage, and absent friends; she tells all the events of life at No. 169 Mulberry-st., first floor, back room. Ladies 25 cents; gents 50 cents. She causes speedy marriage. Charge extra."

Her customers are much more addicted to love than marriage, so that the wedlock clause cannot be relied on to bring many fish to the net, but it is supposed to give an air of respectability to the advertisement.

The Cash Customer was, perhaps, an exception to this general rule, and feeling that he would on the whole rather like a "speedy marriage," and wouldn't so much mind the "extra charge," he went, in cold blood, with this matrimonial intent to the street, found the number, and heroically entered the house in the very face of a threatened unclean baptism from the upper windows.

His timid knock at the door of the room was answered by a sturdy "Come in," from the inside; hat deferentially in hand he modestly entered, and was received by a fat woman with a bust of proportions exceeding those of Mrs. Merdle in "Little Dorrit," and who was attired in a dress which may have been clean in the earlier years of its history, though the supposition is exceedingly apocryphal. This lady pointed to a chair, and then composedly seated herself and resumed her explorations with a comb, in the hair of a vicious boy of about three years old, the eldest scion of Madame Leander.

Her enthusiasm in the cause of entomological science was too ardent to be quenched by the mere presence of an observer, and she continued to hunt her insect prey with all the ardor of a she-Nimrod, and with a zeal that was rewarded by a brilliant success. The youth, over whose fertile head the game seemed to rove and range in countless numbers, was somewhat restless under the operation, and oftentimes disturbed the eager sportswoman by manifesting a desire to run into the street and carry the hunting-ground with him, and was as often recalled to a sense of the proprieties by a few judicious slaps, which he stoically endured without a whimper, being evidently used to it.

This feminine lover of the chase, this Diana of the fiery scalp, looked up from her occupations long enough to say to her visitor that Madame Lent would soon be disengaged. Meantime, he made a careful survey of the premises.

Two chairs, an old lounge with its dingy red cover fastened on with pins, and a trunk covered with an old bit of carpet, were the accommodations for seating visitors. A cooking-stove, and a suspicious-looking wash-bowl which stood in the corner of the room, without a pitcher, were probably for the accommodation of the Madame and the lady with the comb. On the shabby lounge sat a stolid-looking Irish girl, who was waiting her turn to have her fortune told. Having fully comprehended the room and everything in it, the visitor turned his attention to literary pursuits, and thoroughly perused an odd copy of a newspaper that lay invitingly on the table.

Visitors kept dropping in, mostly servant-appearing girls, though there were three women attired in silk and laces, who would have appeared respectable had their faces been hidden and their conversation been suppressed. The lady with the comb and the boy presently departed to some unknown region, and soon returned with a reinforcement of chairs and stools. The number of visitors increased, until, besides the original stranger, nine were waiting. Among others, there came, in a friendly way, but still with a sharp eye to business, a tall woman, attired in a red dress and a purple bonnet, who is the keeper of a well-known house in Sullivan street, and whose name is not strange to the police. An unrestrained business conversation ensued between her and the heroine of the comb, which must have been interesting to the female listeners.

One hour and eleven minutes did the Cash Customer patiently wait before he was admitted to the mysterious conference with the queen of magic. At last, after the man who was at first closeted with her had concluded his inquiries, and the stolid Irish girl had been disposed of, the woman with the suggestive bust beckoned the long-suffering and patient man to follow, and he fearfully entered the sanctum.

The room of conjuration was a closet, dark and dirty, and was lighted by one tallow candle, stuck in a Scotch ale bottle. A number of shabby dresses, bony petticoats, and other mysterious articles of women's gear, hung upon the walls; two weak-kneed chairs, a tattered bit of carpet upon about two feet square of the floor, and a little table covered with a greasy oilcloth, composed the furniture of the mystic cell. The cabalistic paraphernalia was limited, there being nothing but a dirty pack of double-headed cards, a small pasteboard box with some scraps of paper in it, and two kinds of powder in little bottles, like hair-oil pots.

Madame Lent is a woman of medium height, about thirty-five years of age, with light-grey eyes, false teeth, a head nearly bald, and hair, what there is of it, of a bright red. Her manner is hurried and confused, and she has a trick of drawing her upper lip disagreeably up under the end of her nose, which labial distortion she doubtless intends for a smile.

She was robed in a bright-colored plaid dress, a dirty lace collar, and a coarse woollen shawl over her shoulders. Motioning her visitor to one chair, she instantly seated herself in the other, and, without demanding pay in advance, commenced operations. She handed the cards to be cut, and then laying them out in their piles, uttered the following sentences:

"I see that your fortune has been and is quite a curious one. Your cards run rather mixed up, you have been very much worried in your head, you were born under two planets, which means that you have seen a great deal of trouble in your younger days, but you are now getting over it and your cards run to better luck, but it is rather mixed up, your cards run to a lady, she is light-haired and blue-eyed, but she is jealous of you, for sometimes you treat her more kinder and sometimes more harsher, and just now she is in trouble and very much mixed up about you. There is a man of black hair and eyes, a dark-*complected* man who pretends to be your friend and is very fair to your face, but you must beware of him, for he is your secret enemy and will do you an injury if he can; he is trying to get the lady, but I don't think he'll do it, though I don't know, for the thing is so much mixed up—he has deceived you, and the lady has deceived you, they have both deceived you, but now they have got mixed up, and she turns from him with scorn, and seems to like you the best—I don't exactly see how it all is, for it seems rather mixed up like—you must persevere, you must coax her more; you can coax her to do anything, but you can't drive her any more than you can drive that wall—always treat her more kinder and never more harsher, and she will soon be yours entirely—beware of the dark-complected man; you must not talk so much and be so open in your mind, and above all don't talk so much to the dark-complected man, for he seems to worry you, and your affairs and his are all mixed up like."

Here her auditor expressed a desire to know something definite and certain about his future wife, whereupon the red-haired prophetess shuffled the cards again with the following result:

"You will have but one more wife. She will be good and true, and will not be mixed up with any dark-complected man. She will be rich and you will be rich, for your business cards run very smooth, but your marriage cards do not run very close to you, and you will not be married for six or eight months; you will have three children; you will see your future wife within nine hours, nine days, or nine weeks; do not blame me if it runs into the tens, but I tell you it will fall within the nines. Another man is trying to get her away from you, he is a light-complected man, he has had some influence over her, but she now turns from him with disdain, and she will be yours and yours only—things are a little worried and mixed up now, but she will be yours and yours only, the light-complected man can't hurt you. I have something that I can give you that will make her love you tender and true; it will force her to do it and she won't have no power to help herself, but you can do with her just what you please; I charge extra for that."

Here was a chance to procure a love-philtre at a reasonable rate, and unless the dark woman kept that article ready made and done up in packages to suit customers, he could observe the terrible ceremonies with which it was prepared, listen to the spells and incantations with an attent eye, and take mental notes of all the mighty magic. The opportunity was too good to be lost, and he at once signified his desire to try a little of the extra witchcraft, and his willingness to draw on his purse for the requisite amount of ready cash to purchase this gratification of a laudable curiosity.

Madame Lent now assumed an air of the most intense gravity, and shook into a very dirty bit of paper a little white powder from one of the pomatum pots, and a corresponding quantity of grayish powder from pot No. 2, and stirred them carefully together with the tip of her finger. When she had mixed them to her liking she folded the diabolical compound in a small paper. Then she prepared another mixture in the same manner, and made a pretence of adding another ingredient from a little pasteboard box, which probably hadn't had anything in it for a month. Folding this also in a paper she presented them both to her interested guest, with these directions:

"You must shake some of the first powder on your true-love's head, or neck, or arms, if you can, but if you can't manage this, put it on her dress—the other powder you must sprinkle about your room when you go to bed to-night—this will draw her to you, and she will love you and you alone and can't help herself; this will surely operate, if it don't, come and tell me."

One more cabalistic performance and the hocus-pocus was ended. She desired her customer to give her the first letter of his true love's name. He, unabashed by the unexpected demand, with great presence of mind promptly invented a sweetheart on the spot, and extemporized a name for her before the question was repeated. Then the mysterious Madame required his own initial, which, being obtained, she wrote the two on slips of paper with some mystic figures appended, in manner following. E., 17; M., 24. Then she shiveringly whispered:

"You must do as I told you with the powders before eleven o'clock to-night, for between the hours of eleven and twelve I shall boil your name and hers in herbs which will draw her to you, and she can't help herself but will be tender and true, and will be yours and yours only. When she is drawed to you then you must marry her."

The anxious inquirer promised obedience, and agreed to give the powders as per prescription, before the midnight cookery should commence, paid his dollar (fifty cents for the consultation and a like sum for the love-powders), and made his exit with a comprehensive bow, which included the Madame, the bony petticoats, the beer-bottle, and the fast-vanishing remains of the single tallow-candle in one reverential farewell.

CHAPTER XII.

Wherein are inscribed all the particulars of a visit to the "Gipsy Girl," of No. 207, Third Avenue, with an allusion to Gin, and other luxuries dear to the heart of that beautiful Rover.

CHAPTER XII.

THE GIPSY GIRL.

There is much less affectation of high-flown and lofty-sounding names among the ladies of the black-art mysteries, than might very naturally be expected. Most of them are content with plain "Madame" Smith, or unadorned "Mrs." Jones, and "The Gipsy Girl" is almost the only exception to this rule that is to be encountered among all the fortune-tellers of the city.

This arises from no poverty of invention on their part, but from a sound conviction that in this case, simplicity is an element of sound policy. There has been no lack of "mysteriously gifted prophetesses," and of "astonishing star readers;" there have been, I believe, within the last few years, a "Daughter of Saturn," and a "Sorceress of the Silver Girdle;" and once the "Queen of the Seven Mysteries" condescended to sojourn in Gotham for five weeks, but on the whole it has been found that a more modest title pays better. To be sure, the "Daughter of Saturn" was tried for conspiring with two other persons to swindle an old and wealthy gentleman out of seventeen hundred dollars, and the "Queen of the Seven Mysteries" was dispossessed by a constable for non-payment of rent; and these untoward circumstances may have acted as a "modest quencher" on the then growing disposition to indulge in fantastic and romantic appellations.

At this present time "The Gipsy Girl" enjoys almost a monopoly of this sort of thing, and she is by no means constant to one name, but sometimes announces herself as "The Gipsy Woman," "The Gipsy Palmist," and "The Gipsy Wonder," as her whim changes.

This woman has not been in New York years enough to become complicated in as many rascalities as some of her elder sisters in the mystic arts, but her surroundings are of a nature to indicate that she has not been backward in her American education on these points. She has not been remarkably successful in making money, as a witch; not having been educated among the strumpets and gamblers of the city she lacked that extensive acquaintance on going into business, that had secured for her rivals in trade such immediate success. Her fondness for gin has also proved a serious bar to her rapid advancement, and has given not a few of her customers the idea that she is not so eminently trustworthy as one having the control of the destinies of others should be. In fact, she loves her enemy, the bottle, to that extent, that she has many times permitted her devotion to it to interfere seriously with her business, leading her to disappoint customers. The quality of her sober predictions is about the same as that of others in the same profession, but her intoxicated foretellings are deserving of a chapter to themselves, and they shall have it, for from force of peculiar circumstances, which will be explained hereafter, the Cash Customer made three visits to this celebrated woman. Her first address was 207 3d Avenue, between Eighteenth and Nineteenth Streets.

The Gipsy Girl! How romantically suggestive was this feminine phrase to the fancy of an enthusiastic reporter. Was it then, indeed, permitted that he should know Meg Merrilees in private life? His heart danced at the poetic possibility, and his heels would have extemporized a vigorous hornpipe but that his saltatory ardor was quenched by the depressing sturdiness of cow-hide boots. With the most pleasing anticipations he perused the subjoined advertisement again and again, and looked to the happy future with a joyful hope.

"A Wonder—The Gipsy Girl.—If you wish to know all the secrets of your past and future life, the knowledge of which may save you years of sorrow and care, don't fail to consult the above-named palmist. Charge 50 cents. The Gipsy has also on hand a secret which will enable any lady or gentleman to win or obtain the affections of the opposite sex. Charge extra. No. 207 3d av., between 18th and 19th sts."

How the knowledge of all the secrets of his past life was to save him years of sorrow and care at this late day he could not exactly comprehend, and was willing to pay fifty cents for the information. And then wasn't it worth half a dollar to see a live gipsy? Of course it was.

Kettles, camp-fires, white tents under green trees, indigenous brown babies and exotic white ones, with a panorama of empty cradles and mourning mothers in the distance, moonlight nights, midnight foraging excursions, expeditions against impertinent game-keepers, demonstrations against hen-roosts—successful by masterly generalship and pure strategic science—and the midnight forest cookery of contraband game, surreptitious pigs and clandestine chickens—were among the romantic ideas of a delightful vagabond gipsy life that at once suggested themselves to the mind of the Cash Customer. He did not really expect to find the Third-Avenue gipsy camped out under a bed-quilt tent in the lee of the house, or cooking her dinner in an iron pot over an out-door fire in the back yard, but he had a vague undefined hope that there would be some visible indications of gipsy life, if it was nothing more than the pawn-tickets for stolen spoons.

He thought to find at least one or two beautiful babies knocking about, decorated with coral necklaces and golden clasps, suggestive of rich parents and better days, and had firmly resolved to send the little innocents to the alms-house by way of improving their condition. Full of these romantic notions, the reporter started on his philanthropic mission, taking the preliminary precaution of leaving at home his watch and pocket-book, and carrying with him only small change enough to pay the advertised charges.

In one of those three-story brick houses so abounding in this city, which seem to have been built by the mile and cut off in slices to suit purchasers, in the

Third Avenue above Eighteenth Street, dwelt at that time the gay Bohemian. The building in which she lived, though three stories in height, is very short between joints, which style of architecture makes all the rooms low and squat, as if somebody had shut the house into itself like a telescope, and had never pulled it out again.

Out of the chimney, which was the little end of the telescope, issued a sickly smoke; and through a door in the lower story, which was the big end thereof, was the stranger admitted by a little girl. This girl was, probably, a pure article of gipsy herself originally, but had been so much adulterated by partial civilization that she combed her hair daily and submitted to shoes and stockings without a murmur. Ragged indeed was this reclaimed wanderer; saucy and dirty-faced was this sprouting young maiden, but she was sharp-witted, and scented money as quickly as if she had been the oldest hag of her tribe; so she asked her customer to walk up stairs, which he did. She herself went up stairs with a skip and a whirl, showed her visitor into the grand reception room with a gyrating flourish, and disappeared in a "courtesy" of so many complex and dizzy rotations that she seemed to the eyes of the bewildered traveller to evaporate in a red flannel mist. As soon as she had spun herself out of sight he recovered his presence of mind and looked about him.

The romantic gipsy who sojourned here had tried to furnish her rooms like civilized people, doubtless out of respect to her many patrons. A thread-bare carpet was under foot; a little parlor stove with a little fire in it was standing on a little piece of zinc, and did its little utmost to heat the room; an uncomfortable looking sofa covered with shabby and faded red damask graced one side of the apartment, and a lounge, of curtailed dimensions, partially covered with shreds of turkey red calico, adorned another side.

This latter article of furniture, with its tattered cover, through which suspicious bits of curled hair peeped out, and wide crevices in its rickety frame were plainly visible, looked much too suggestive of cockroaches and other insect delicacies of the season to be an inviting place of repose.

Three chairs were dispersed throughout the room, on one of which the reporter bestowed himself, and the rest of the furniture consisted of a table, so exceedingly shaky and sensitive in the joints that it might have been the grim skeleton of some former table, loosely hung together with unseen wires; and a cheap looking-glass that had suffered so serious a comminuted fracture as to be past all surgery—this was all except some little plaster images of saints, strangers to the Cash Customer, and a black rosary, which article would seem to show that efforts had been put forth to Christianize this nut-brown gipsy maid.

A clinking of glasses was heard in the adjoining apartment, then the door was opened with an independent flirt, and the gay Bohemian appeared on the scene.

If it were desired to fancy visions of enchanting loveliness it would be necessary to insert therein other ingredients than the gipsy girl of the Third Avenue; alone she would be insufficient; too much would be left to the imagination; and in any event the illusion would be too great to last long.

She is of medium height, her eyes are brown and bright, and her hands are very large and red. She has no hair, but wears a scratch red wig, which gives her head a utilitarian character. Her face is deeply pitted with the small-pox, more than pitted—gullied, scarred, and seamed, as though some jealous rival had been trying to plough her complexion under; little short light hairs are thinly scattered on her cheek bones and upper lip, and in the shadows of the little ridges that disease had left, irresistibly compelling the mind to make an absurd comparison of her face with a sterile field, and imagine that at some past day it had been spaded up to plant a beard, which had only grown in scanty patches, here and there. Her nails were horny and ill-shaped, and underneath them and at their roots were large deposits of dirt and other fertilizing compounds, under the stimulating influence of which they had grown lank and long. Her attire was a sort of cross between the picturesque wildness of the gipsy, and the more civilized and unbecoming dress of Third Avenue Christians.

She was apparelled, principally, in a red flannel jacket, and a check handkerchief, which was passed under her chin and tied on the top of her wig, where the knot looked like a blue butterfly. There was a gown, but a series of subsoiling experiments would have been necessary to determine the material and texture; the surface was palpably dirt. Accompanying her there was a strong smell of gin, and from the odor of the liquor the visitor judged that it was a very poor article.

This gay old gipsy drew a chair to the table, and sat down, not in a graceful and composed manner, but more as if she had been dumped from a cart. She soon partially recovered herself, and straightened up slightly from the heap into which she had collapsed, and, turning her head away from her customer, she elaborately remarked: "Fifty cents and your left 'and."

The Individual made a careful search for his small change, and fished out the exact amount which he promptly paid over.

This delightful gipsy then took his left hand and looked at it for a minute in an imbecile kind of way, as if she didn't know exactly what to do with it, and was undecided whether it was to be made into soup, or she was to drink it immediately with warm water and a little sugar. This last impression evidently prevailed, for she tried to pour it into her apron, and only recovered from her delusion when the fingers tangled themselves up in the strings. Then a glimmering of the true state of the case seemed to dawn upon her, and she began to have a dim idea that she was expected to say something.

Now the roving gipsy was not by any means intoxicated at this time; that is to say, she may have been partaking of gin, or gin and water, or may have been sucking sugar that had gin on it, or she may have been taking a little gin and peppermint for a stomach-ache, or she may have been bathing her head in gin, or have been otherwise making use of that potent remedy as a medicine, but she was by no means a subject for official interference in case she had wandered into the street, but she was, to tell the truth, not in her most clear-headed condition; although probably she did not see more than one Cash Customer sitting solemnly before her, still that one was quite as many as she could well manage at that time.

After the signal failure of her little demonstration on the hand of her guest, she, by a strong effort, seemed to concentrate her faculties, and after several trials she roused herself and spoke as follows, emphasizing the short words with spiteful vindictiveness, and paying the most particular attention to the improper aspiration of the h's.

"You *are* a person as *has* seen a great deal *of* dif—"

The gay Bohemian here evidently desired to say "difficulty," but the word was a sad stumbling-block, a four-syllable rock ahead which was too much for her powers in her then exhausted state of mind; she charged on the unfortunate word boldly, however, and tried to carry it by storm, but each time was repulsed with great loss of breath—"a great deal of dif—dif—dif—diffle"—it was no use, so she tried back and began again.

"You *are* a man as *has* seen a great deal of *diffleculency*," was what she said, but it didn't seem to satisfy her, so she tried again, and after a number of trials she hit a happy medium between "*dif*" and "*diffleculency*" and compromised on "*difflety*," which useful addition to the language she took occasion to repeat as often as possible with an air of decided triumph.

"You *are* a man as *has* seen a great deal of difflety *and* trouble—I would not go *to* say you 'ave been through too much difflety *and* trouble, still you 'ave seen difflety *and* trouble. If you had been a luckier man *in* your past life you *would* not 'ave seen *so* much difflety and trouble, still you *'ave* seen difflety *and* trouble—I 'ope you will not see so much difflety *and* trouble *in* the future—Life: you *will* live long; you will live *to* be 69 years of *hage and will* die of a lingering disease—you *will* be sick for a long time, and *will* not suffer much difflety and trouble—sixty-nine years of *hage* you *will* live to be—Death: don't think *of* death; that is *too* far hoff a you *to* think of—but you *will* die when you *are* 69 years of hage, and you *may* 'ope to go right hup to 'eaven, for you *will* 'ave no more difflety and trouble then—Money: you *will* 'ave money, and you *will* 'ave plenty of money, but you must not look for money until *you* 'ave reached your middle *hage*—a distant Hinglish relative of yours *will* leave you money, but you *will* 'ave difflety *and* trouble in getting it; do not hexpect *to* get *this* money without difflety, no do not cherish *such* a 'ope—hit *will* be *in* the 'ands of a man who wont hanswer your letters nor take notice of your happlications, you *will* 'ave *to* cross the hocean yourself; this money *will* be a good deal of money *and* will make *you* 'appy for the rest *of* your days—Business: you *will* thrive in business, you *will* never be hunfortunate in business, you *will* 'ave luck in business, you will always *do* a good business, may hexpect to make money *by* large speculations in business; difflety *and* trouble in business you *will* not know—Great

Troubles: you need not hexpect to 'ave many great troubles *for* you will not; you 'ave 'ad your great troubles *in* your hearly days—Sickness: you *will* never see no sickness, 'ave no fear of sickness for you *will* not see none; sickness, do not care for it and make your mind *heasy*—Friends: you 'ave *got* many friends, both 'ere and helsewhere, your friends *will* be 'appy and you will be 'appy, there will be no difflety *and* trouble between you, you 'ave 'ad trouble with your friends, but you face brighter days, be 'appy—Wives: you *will* 'ave *but* one wife; in the third month *from* now you *will* 'ear from 'er, you *will* get a letter from 'er, and in the fourth month you *will* be married—she is not particularly 'andsome, nor she *is* not specially hugly, she 'as got blue heyes and brown 'air, *is* partickler fond of 'ome and is now heighteen years of hage—'Appiness: you *will* be the 'appiest people in *all* the land, you can't himagine the 'appiness you *will* 'ave—Children: you *will* 'ave three children, after you are married you *will* see no more difflety *and* trouble; you *will* die *in* a foreign land across the hocean but you *will* die 'appy. 'Ope for 'appiness and 'ave *no* huneasiness."

Thus prophesied the gay Bohemian, the nut-brown maid, the dark-eyed oracle, the wise charmer, the female seer, the beautiful sibyl, the lovely enchantress, the romantic "gipsy girl" of the Third Avenue.

Romance and poesy were effectually demolished by the overpowering realities of dirt, vulgarity, cockneyism, ignorance, scratch-wigs, bad English, and bad gin. Sadly the Individual walked down stairs behind the gyrating girl, who reappeared with an agile pirouette, twirled down on her toes, and opened the door with a dizzy revolution that made her look as if her head and shoulders had got into a whirlpool of petticoats, and were past all hope of mortal rescue. The little chink, as of a bottle and glass, came faintly from the apartment which is the home of the gipsy, and the individual fancied that the gay Bohemian had returned to her devotions.

CHAPTER XIII.

Contains a true account of the Magic Establishment of Mrs. Fleury, of No. 263 Broome Street, and also shows the exact quantity of Witchcraft that snuffy personage can afford for one Dollar.

CHAPTER XIII.

MADAME FLEURY, No. 263 BROOME STREET.

From what the reader has already perused of the predictions and prophecies of these modern dealers in magic, he will hardly think them of a character to inspire any great degree of confidence in the minds of people of ordinary common sense. Still less will he be disposed to believe that merchants of "credit and renown;" business men, engaged in occupations, the operations of which are presumed to be governed by the nicest mathematical calculations, are ever so far influenced by the miserable jargon of these "fortune-tellers," as to seriously consult them in business matters of great importance.

Such, however, is the humiliating truth.

There are in New York city a number of merchants, bankers, brokers, and other persons eminent in the business world, and respectable in all social relations, who never make an important business move in any direction, until after consultation with one or another of the Witches of New York.

There are many who are regular periodical customers, and who visit the shrine of the oracle once a month, or once in six weeks, as regularly as they make out their balance-sheets, or take an account of stock, and who guide their future investments and business ventures as much by the written fifty-cent prophecy as by either of the other documents.

Many country merchants have also learned this trick, and some of them are in constant correspondence with the cheap sybils of Grand Street; and others, when they come to the city for their stock of goods for the next half year, visit their chosen fortune-teller and get full and explicit directions how to conduct their business for the coming six months. Of course, these proceedings are conducted with the greatest possible secrecy, and the attention of the writer was first awakened to this fact by the indiscreet boastings of certain ones of the witches themselves, who are not a little proud of their influence, and after observations afforded ample proof and corroboration of all he had been told.

Great money enterprises have without doubt been seriously affected by the yea or nay of the Bible and key, and perhaps the Atlantic Cable Company would have received more hearty assistance, and its stock more extensive subscriptions in Wall Street, if certain ones of the fortune-tellers had possessed more faith in its success, and had so advised their patrons.

Incredible as these statements may seem, they are nevertheless true, and this fact is another proof that gross superstition is not confined to the low and filthy parts of the city, where rags and dirt are the universal rule, but that it has likewise a thrifty growth in quarters of the town where stand the palaces of the "merchant princes," and in avenues where rags are almost unknown, and broadcloth, and gold, and fine-twined linen are the common wear.

It is said that certain counsel eminent in the learned profession of the law, and that certain even of the judges of the bench, have been known to consult the female practicers of the Black Art, but the author has never been personally cognizant of a case of this kind, and has no means of knowing whether the consultation was intended to benefit the lawyer or the witch; whether the former desired enlightenment as to the management of some knotty professional point, or whether the latter wanted legal advice as to some of the side branches of her business.

Mrs. Fleury, whose domicile and mode of procedure are described in this present chapter, has a large run of this sort of what may be termed *respectable* custom, and she does not fail to profit by it to the utmost. She came to New York, from France, about six or seven years ago, and at once established herself in the witch business, which she could advertise extensively in the papers, although the other branches of her profession, by which she probably makes more money than by telling fortunes, would by no means bear newspaper publicity. What these other branches are, is more explicitly stated in other chapters of this book, and, in fact, needs to be but hinted at, to be at once understood by nearly all who read.

Madame Fleury advertised the world of her arrival in America, and of her supernatural powers, and in a short time customers began to flock in. It is now her boast that she has as "respectable a connexion" as any one in the trade, and that she has as great a number of "regular, reliable customers," as any conjuress in America. She says that most of her "regular customers" visit her once in six weeks, six being with her a favorite number, and she not undertaking to guarantee her *business* predictions for a greater length of time.

Whether she makes any discount from her ordinary prices to these regular traders, she did not state, but probably witchcraft is governed by the same rule as other commodities, and comes cheaper to wholesale dealers.

Duly armed and equipped with staff and scrip, and duly fortified within by such stimulants as the exigencies of the case seemed to demand, the Cash Customer set out for 263 Broome Street, and after strict trial and due examination of the premises and the people, he made the following report.

It was a favorite remark of a learned though mistaken philosopher of the olden time, that "you can't make a whistle of a pig's tail." The philosopher died, but his saying was accepted by the world as an axiom— a bit of incontrovertible truth, eternal, Godlike, fully up to par, worth a hundred per cent., with no possibility of discount. Time, however, which often demonstrates the fallibility of human wisdom, has not spared even this oft-quoted adage; and now there is not a collection of curiosities in the land which lacks a pig-tail whistle to proclaim in the shrillest tones the falsity of the wise man's proposition, and the triumph of Yankee ingenuity. Had this same philosopher been interrogated on the subject, he would undoubtedly have announced, and with an equal show of probability on his side of the argument, that "you can't make a star-reading prophetess out of a snuffy old woman;" but had he lived to the present day, the Cash Customer would have taken great pleasure in exhibiting to him these two apparently irreconcilable characters combined in a single person, and that person Mrs. Fleury, who pays for the daily insertion of the following advertisement in the newspapers.

"ASTROLOGY.—Mrs. Fleury, from Paris, is the most celebrated lady of the present age, in telling future events, true and certain. She answers questions on business, marriage, absent friends, &c., by magnetism. Office No. 263 Broome-st."

There is not so much of promise in this paragraph, as there is in some of the more grandiloquent announcements of the other witches—not probably, that Madame Fleury is any less pretentious than they, but her knowledge of the English language is not perfect enough to enable her to give her ideas their full effect.

The Cash Customer resolved to visit this "most celebrated lady of the age," who had come all the way from Paris, to tell his "future events true and certain," nothing daunted by the circumstance that she lives in the filthiest part of Broome Street, which has never been swept clean since it was a very new Broome indeed.

If our fancy farmers, who expend so much money upon the various foreign manures and fertilizing compounds, would but turn their eyes in the direction of Broome Street, a single glance would convince them of the inexhaustible resources of their own country, while guano would instantly depreciate in value, and the island of Ichaboe not be worth a quarrel. This prolific and valuable deposit that covers Broome Street bears perennial crops: in the spring and summer, dirty-faced children and mean-looking dogs seem to spring from it spontaneously; they are succeeded during the colder weather by a crop of tumble-down barrels, and cast-away broken carts; while the humbler and more insignificant things, the uncared for weeds, so to speak, of the abundant harvest, such as potato parings, and fish heads, and shreds of ragged dish-cloths, and bits of broken crockery, and old bones, are in season all the year round.

In the midst of this filth, with policy-shops adjacent, and pawnbrokers' offices close at hand, and rum shops convenient in the neighborhood—where the reeking streets and stagnant gutters, and the heaps of decomposing garbage, send up a stench so thick and heavy that it beslimes everything it touches, and makes a man feel as if he were far past the saving powers of soap and soft water, and was fast dissolving into rancid lard oil—in this congenial atmosphere flourishes the prophetess, and here is found the mansion of Mrs. Fleury, "the most celebrated lady of the age in telling future events." Her mansion is not one that would be selected as a permanent residence by any one with a superabundance of cash capital, nor did it seem quite suited to the deservings of the "most celebrated lady of the present age;" the house, a three-story brick, originally intended to be something above the common, has been for so many years misused and badly treated by reckless tenants, that it has completely lost its good temper, as well as its good looks, and is now in a perpetual state of aggravated sulkiness. It resents the presence of a stranger as an impertinent intrusion, and avenges the personality in various disagreeable ways. It twitches its rickety stairways impatiently under his feet, as if to shake him off and damage him by the fall—it viciously attempts to pinch and jam his fingers with moody dogged doors, which hold back as long as they can, and then close with a sudden snap, exceedingly dangerous to the unwary—it tears his clothes with ambushed rusty nails, and unsuspected hooks, and sharp and jagged splinters—it creaks its floors under his tread with a doleful whine, and complains of his cruel treatment in sharp-pointed, many-cornered tears of plaster, which it drops from the ceiling upon his head the instant he takes his hat off—it yawns its wide cellar doors open like a greedy mouth, evidently hoping that an unlucky step will pitch him headlong down—and it conducts itself in a thousand ill-natured ways like a sulky child that has been waked up too early in the morning, and not properly whipped into good behavior. The Individual, however, entered the doors, unabashed by the malignant scowl which was visible all over the face of the unamiable mansion, and stumbled through a narrow, dirty hall, up two flights of groaning stairs, before he discovered any sign of the whereabouts of Madame. She evidently did not occupy the entire of this sulky edifice, or he would have seen some of the servants or retainers, who would have been only too happy to direct him to the head-quarters of the sorceress. But the few people he saw about the place seemed to be each one occupied with his or her own private affairs, and to be too much taken up therewith to pay the slightest attention to the new-comer. Their attentions to each other were confined to reproaches, uncomplimentary assertions, and sundry maledictory remarks, accompanied, in case of the younger members of the various tribes, with pinches, pokes, punches, and small but frequent showers of brickbats.

The Individual disregarded these evidences of good feeling, not considering himself called upon to reply to any which were not addressed to him individually, and plodded on till his roving eye rested on a tin sign, on which was inscribed, "Madame Fleury, Room No. 4." There were no mysterious emblems or cabalistic flourishes accompanying this simple announcement.

He pulled the knob and the door was instantly opened by the lady herself, so quickly that the bell had no time to ring until all necessity for it was over—she had evidently heard the advancing footsteps of her customer, and had stood ready to pounce upon him. She ushered him into the apartment, where he soon recovered his self-possession, and took an observation.

The room was a small square one, shabbily furnished with very few articles of furniture, and these were dimly visible through the snuffy mist which filled the apartment; there was snuff everywhere; there was a snuffy dust on the chairs; there was a precipitate of snuff on the floor, and, if snuff was capable of crystallization, there would undoubtedly have been stalactitic formations of snuff depending from the ceiling; the Madame herself was snuff-colored, as if she had been boiled in a decoction of tobacco.

She is a Frenchwoman, and has had about half a century's experience of her present fleshly tabernacle, which is somewhat the worse for wear, although from the fossil remains of bygone beauty, still visible in her ancient countenance, her customer inclined to the belief that in some remote age she was comely and pleasant to the eye. He founded this hypothesis upon the brown hair and hazel eyes which time has spared.

In respect to personal cleanliness, the Individual regrets to say that the Madame was not in every respect what a critical observer would wish to see; her hands and arms were in a condition which would naturally lead to the belief that the Croton Corporation had cut off the water; and under each of her finger-nails was a dark-colored deposit, which may have been snuff, but looked like something dirtier. She was dressed in a light striped calico dress, over which was a black velvet mantle trimmed with fur, and on her head was a portentous head-dress which was fearfully and wonderfully made of shabby black lace; her face was in the same condition as her hands and arms, as was also her neck, which was only visible to the upper edge of the collar-bone—further deponent saith not.

She more nearly approached the Cash Customer's notion of the Witch of Endor, than any other lady he had ever heard mentioned in polite society. She at once prepared for business.

She seated herself behind a small stand, dusty with snuff, on which were a number of little books on astrology, written in French and German, and as dirty and as fragrant as if they had been some kind of clumsy vegetable which had been grown in a tobacco plantation.

She asked her visitor if he spoke French or German, to which he replied that, had he been conversant with all the languages invented at the Babel smash-up, he would on this occasion, for particular reasons, prefer to confine himself to English. He also ventured an inquiry as to terms, upon which she produced a card containing a list of her charges, printed in English, French, and German. He learned from this dingy document that the prices of telling fortunes by lines of the hand, by cards, and by the stars, varied in amount from one to five dollars. The Individual concluded that one dollar's worth would suffice, and, approaching the little table, he announced the result of his cogitations. The enchantress, who was so saturated with snuff and tobacco that every time her customer looked her in the face he sneezed, then brought a pack of very filthy cards, which were covered over with mysterious hieroglyphics done in black paint. She asked her visitor to "cut" them, which he reverently though daintily did, whereupon she laid them on the table before her in four rows, and spoke, having previously explained that she used no witchcraft but did all her wonders by the signs of the zodiac. The Individual concentrated his attention, and listened with all his ears while the witch of Broome Street spoke thus:

"I will tell you first what these cards indicate, then I will look at the lines of your hand, and then I will answer three questions."

Here she paused, while her agitated listener sneezed a couple of times; then she resumed, speaking with a strong foreign accent:

"You are good disposition—have excellent memory, you don't have many enemy, but what you do is of your own sex—you are very frank person and you was born in the sign of the Crab. You have some lucky days which are Mondays, Thursdays, and Fridays, whatever you do on these days is well, but you shall not wash your hair on Thursdays, if so, you will wash all your luck away. You must be very careful of fire and water, you will be in great danger of fire and water and you must be very careful. You may die by fire or water, I cannot say but you must certain be very careful of fire and water. You must also be very careful of dogs, very careful of dogs, you may die by a dog, but you must certain be very careful of dogs."

Here she paused again, and while her visitor was meditating on the full force of what he had heard, and was inwardly resolving to go immediately home, shoot Juno, and drown her as-yet-unoffending-but-in-after-days-dangerous-to-his-peace-of-mind-and-the-happiness-of-his-life pups, she prepared for the second portion of her discourse.

Taking the Individual's hand in hers, a proceeding which made him feel as if he had put his fingers into a bladder of Maccoboy, she made the following prediction: "You will be the father of five children, two of them will be boys, who will be a great comfort to you when you grow old."

She spoke no good of the girls, and the customer foresaw feminine trouble in his household with those same young ladies. Having a few moments to himself before she resumed, he worked himself into a great passion with the ungrateful hussies who were about to treat their kind old father in so scandalous a manner; but presently recollecting that they were as yet in the condition of "your sister, Betsey Trotwood, who never was born," he felt that he was slightly premature in his wrath, so he cooled down and resolved to make the best of it with his comfortable boys.

The yellow sorceress continued: "Your line of life is long, and you will live to a good old age. You have had much trouble in love affairs, and now your first love is entirely lost to you. You can never reclaim her, and you must never venture anything in lotteries."

Whether Madame Fleury supposed that her visitor intended to spend his salary in lottery tickets, in the hope of winning back his early love, or whether she supposed that the woman then exhibiting herself as "Perham's Gift Lady," was the person, is not in evidence; but, from the peculiar construction of her last remark, something of the kind must have been in her thoughts. She had now reached the third part of her discourse, and come to the "three questions." She produced an old French Bible, dingy with age and snuff, and which she informed the observer had been in her family for three hundred years; an old iron key was tied between the leaves, with the ring and part of the shank of the key projecting, and the Bible was tightly bound round with many folds of black ribbon. Making her visitor hold one side of the ring of the key, while she held the other, she said: "Ask your three questions, and if they are to be answered in the affirmative the book will turn."

The Individual, who had been much impressed by her canine observation of a few minutes before, and whose thoughts were still running upon his pet Juno, and her six innocent offspring, in a fit of absence of mind propounded this interrogatory:

"Shall I marry the person of whom I am now thinking?" The potent enchantress repeated the question aloud in French, and then, with pale lips and trembling voice, she addressed the book and key thus:

"Holy Bible, I ask you, in the name of the Father, the Son, and the Holy Ghost, will this man marry the person now in his mind?"—then she closed her eyes for a moment, placed one hand over her heart, and rapidly muttered something in so low a tone that it was inaudible to her listener. Immediately the Bible commenced to turn slowly towards her, and soon had made a complete revolution, thus expressing a very decided affirmative.

Having started a matrimonial subject with so satisfactory a result, her customer thought he could do no better than to follow it up, and accordingly asked question No. 2:

"If I marry this person, will the marriage be a happy one?" The same answer was given, in the same manner. Being now satisfied as to his own matrimonial prospects, he concluded to ascertain those of his children, and question No. 3 was asked, as follows:

"Shall I live to see my children happily married?"

There was a long delay, which was undoubtedly occasioned by the difficulty of properly providing for those refractory girls, but at last there came a reluctant "Yes."

Having now got all that his dollar entitled him to, the customer prepared to depart. The Madame informed him that in a few days she would have her "*Magic Mirror*" from Paris, with which she could do new wonders, and she hoped that he would soon call again, adding, "If I was ten year younger I would not admit gentlemen, but now I am old and I must."

CHAPTER XIV.

Describes an interview with the "Cullud" Seer, Mr. Grommer, of No. 34 North Second Street, Williamsburgh, and what that respectable Whitewasher and Prophet told his Visitor.

CHAPTER XIV.

A BLACK PROPHET, MR. GROMMER, No. 34 NORTH SECOND STREET, WILLIAMSBURGH.

Besides those who advertise in the daily journals, there are many other witches in and about the city who do not deign so to inform the world of their miraculous powers. Either they have not full faith in their own supernatural gifts, or they distrust the policy of advertising; at any rate they are only known to the inquiring stranger by accidental rumors, and mysterious side-whisperings emanating from those credulous ones who have had ocular proof of the miracle-working facility of these veiled prophets.

In certain of the older States of the Union, there cannot probably be found any country village that does not boast its old crones of fortune-telling celebrity—women who are not named by the awe-struck youngsters of the town, but with low breath and a startled sort of look thrown backward over the shoulder every minute as if in half-fear that the evil eye is even there upon them. And in almost every neighborhood in any part of the country, there will be one or more old women who delight in mystifying the young folks by telling fortunes in tea-cups, by means of the ominous settling of the "grounds;"—or who, sometimes, even "run the cards," or aspire to read the fates by the portentous turning of the Bible and key. All these conjurations are given without money and without price in the rural districts, but they sometimes work no little mischief.

There people do not advertise their willingness to read the fates, and only exercise their gifts in that direction as a matter of friendship to certain favored ones. The city and the suburbs are full of people of this kind, who profess to know the gift of prophecy and of miracles, but who do not make their whole living by the exercise of their supernatural powers, depending in part on some popular branch of industry. They differ, however, from their sisters of the country in this regard; whenever they do consent to do a little magic for the accommodation of an anxious inquirer, they are very careful to charge him a round price for it. Many of them combine fortune-telling with hard work, and do their full day's work of faithful toil at some legitimate employment, and in the evening amuse themselves with witchcraft.

These are chrysalis witches; prophets in embryo; magicians in a state of apprenticeship; they are learning the trade, and as soon as they feel competent to do journey-work, they drop their hard labor, and at once set up for full-fledged witches or conjurors.

Mr. Grommer, the Black Sage of Williamsburgh, and his solid and amiable wife, were in this half-way state when they were visited by the Cash Customer. Their fame had reached his ears by the means of some kind friends who were cognisant of his peculiar investigations at that time, and who told him of the supernatural gifts of this amiable old couple.

Accordingly the Individual, having made exact inquiries as to their local habitation, one fine morning set out in pursuit, and in due time made up the following report. Since that time it is reported that this worthy pair have followed the law of progression hereinbefore hinted at, and having arrived at the fulness of all magical knowledge, have laid aside the whitewash pail and discarded the scrubbing-brush, and given their time entirely to the practice of the Black Art.

The Individual beginneth his discourse thus:—

It is an old saying, that "The Devil is never so black as he is painted." What may be the precise shade of the complexion of his amiable majesty the Cash Customer has no means of ascertaining to an exact nicety at this present time of writing; but he makes the positive assertion, that some of the Satanic human employees are so black as to need no painting of any description.

Whether or not the ancient "wise men from the East" were swarthy skinned he is not competent to decide; but he is able to prove, by ocular demonstration, to an unbelieving sceptic, that some of the modern "wise men" are particularly "dark-complected."

Mrs. Grommer, of No. 34 North Second Street, in the suburb of Williamsburgh, is a case in point. The fame of this illustrious ebony lady had gone abroad through the land, and her skill in prophecy had been vouched for by those who professed to have personal knowledge of the truthfulness of her predictions. But an air of mystery surrounded the sable sorceress, and it was declared to be impossible to obtain a knowledge of her exact whereabouts, except by a preliminary visit to a certain mysterious "cave," the locality of which was accurately described.

A cave! this promised well; no other witches encountered by the Cash Customer, had he found in a cave, or in anything resembling that hollow luxury.

A cave! the very word smacked of diabolism, and had the true flavor of genuine witchcraft. Our overjoyed hero thought of the Witch of Vesuvius in her mountain cavern—of her lank, grey, dead hair; her livid, corpse-like skin; her stony eye; her shrivelled, blue lips; her hollow voice, and her threatening arm, and skinny, menacing forefinger—of the red-eyed fox at her side, the crested serpent at her feet, the mystic lamp above her head, and the statue in the background, triple-headed with skulls of dog, and horse, and boar. Something of this kind he hoped to witness in the present instance, for he argued that any sorceress who lived in a cave must surely be supplied with some more cabalistic instruments with which to work her spells than greasy playing-cards or rusty brass door-keys. At last, then, he had discovered something in modern witchcraft worthy the ancient romance of the name. Triumphant and overjoyed, he prepared for the visit, confident in his ability to witness any spectacle, however terrible, without flinching, and in his courage to pass any ordeal, however fearful. He swallowed no countercharms or protective potions, and did not even take the precaution to sew a horse-shoe in the seat of his pantaloons.

It is true he was rash, but much must be forgiven to youthful curiosity, especially when conjoined with professional ambition. The carelessness, in respect to his own safety, was productive of no ill effects, for he returned from this perilous excursion in every regard as good as he went. He had by this time entirely recovered from his matrimonial aspirations, and had given up all hope of a witch wife. Still, he hoped to find in the *cave*, something more worthy the ancient and honorable name of witchcraft than anything he had yet seen.

Alas! for the uncertainty of mortal hopes. All is vanity, bosh, and botheration.

On arriving at the enchanted spot, it soon became evident to the senses of our astonished friend that the "Cave" was not a cavern, fit for the habitation of a powerful sorceress, but was merely a mystifying cognomen applied to a drinking saloon with a billiard room attached, which had accommodations, also, for persons who wished to participate in other profane games.

On entering the "Cave," your deluded customer saw no toothless hag with the expected witch-like surroundings, but observed only a company of men, seemingly respectable, indulging in plentiful potations of beer and certain other liquids, which appeared, at the distance from which he observed them, to be the popular compounds designated in the vulgar tongue as "whiskey toddies." Addressing the nearest bystander, the gulled Individual ascertained the habitation of Mrs. Grommer, and immediately departed in search of that interesting female.

The way was crooked, as all Williamsburgh ways are, but after an irregular, curvilinear journey of half an hour, the anxious inquirer stood in front of the looked-for mansion.

The grading of the street has left at this point a gravel bank some six or eight feet high, on the summit of which is perched the house of Mrs. Grommer, like a contented mud-turtle on a sunny stump. It is a one-story affair, with several irregular wings or additions sprouting out of it at unexpected angles, and, on the whole, it looks as if it had been originally built tall and slim like a tallow candle, but had melted and run down into its present indescribable shape. The architect neglected to provide this beautiful edifice with a front door, and the inquirer was compelled to ascend the bank by a flight of rheumatic steps, and make a grand detour through currant bushes, chickens, washtubs, rain-barrels, and colored children, irregular as to size, and variegated as to hue, to the back, and only door. Here his modest rap was unanswered, and he composedly walked in, unasked, through the kitchen, and took a seat in the parlor, where he was presently discovered by the lady of the house, but not until he had time to take an accurate observation.

Mrs. Grommer had, up to this time, been engaged in making a public example of certain ones of her grandchildren, who had been trespassing on the currant bushes of a neighbor, and had been caught in the act. Their indulgent grandmother, being scandalized by this exhibition of youthful depravity, with a regard for the demands of strict justice that did her infinite credit, had inflicted on several of the delinquents that mild punishment known as "spanking." The novelty of the sight had drawn together quite a collection of the neighbors, who signified their approval of the deed by encouraging cheers.

Meantime the Individual had ample time to contemplate the inside beauties of the mansion of the sable prophet. Mrs. Grommer soon finished her athletic exercise out-doors, and came into the house to rearrange her dress and receive her company.

The reception-room was about 10 by 12, and so low that a tall man could not yawn in it without rapping his head against the ceiling. In places the plaster had been displaced and the bare lath showed through, reminding one of skeletons. The floor was dingily carpeted; a double bed occupied one side of the room, a small cooking-stove stood in the middle of the floor and had a disproportionately slim pipe issuing out of the corner, like a straw in a mint-julep; seven chairs of varied patterns, a small round table, on which lay a pack of cards covered with a cloth, and a tumble-down chest of drawers completed the necessary furniture of the apartment. The ornaments are quickly enumerated. A black wooden cross hung by the windows, a few cheap and gaudy Scriptural prints were fastened against the wall, a chemist's bottle, of large dimensions, and filled with a blue liquid, reposed on the chest of drawers, side by side with a few miniature casts of lambs and dogs; and on a little shelf stood a quarter-size plaster bust of some unknown worthy, of which the head had been knocked off and its place significantly supplied with a goose-egg.

In a short time Mrs. Grommer emerged from an unlooked-for apartment and entered the room. She is a negress and a grandmother—her age is 65, and a brood of children, together with a swarm of the aforesaid grandchildren, reside near at hand and keep the old lady's mansion constantly besieged.

As to size—she is large, apparently solid, and would struggle severely with a 200 pound weight before she would acknowledge herself conquered. She was neatly attired, and, in fact, a most grateful air of cleanliness pervaded the entire establishment, and it was a refreshing contrast to most of the dens of the fairer-skinned witches heretofore encountered by the cash delegate.

The sable one entered into conversation, and a few minutes were passed in cheerful chat, in the course of which she thus referred to the scapegrace husband of one of her numerous daughters: "They think Anson is dead, but I can't station him dead. I think he's at sea somewhere, or in a foreign land, but I can't station him dead. He might as well be under ground for all the good he is, for he is such a poor, mis'able, drinkin' feller that he aint no use, but, after all, I can't run him dead."

At last, the object of the visit was mentioned, and, to the individual's great surprise, Mrs. Grommer positively and peremptorily refused to give him the benefit of her prophetic powers.

She said: "It aint no use; I never does for gentlemen. I does sometimes for ladies, but I can't do it for gentlemen." Remonstrance and entreaty were alike useless; she was immovable. At last, she said she would call her "old man," who could tell fortunes as well as she could, but she added, with a determined shake of the head: "He'll do it, but he will charge you a dollar; and he wont do it under, neither." When her hearer expressed his willingness to learn his future fate by the masculine medium, she addressed him thus: "You station there, in that chair, and I'll send him." The disappointed one "stationed" in the designated chair, and awaited the coming of the "old man." He soon appeared and seated himself, ready to begin.

"Old Man" Grommer is a professor of the whitewashing branch of decorative art. He occasionally relaxes his noble mind from the arduous mental labor attendant upon the successful carrying on of his regular business, and condescends to earn an easy dollar by fortune-telling. He is a shrewd-looking old man, with a dash of white blood in his composition; his hair curls tightly all over his head, but is elaborated on each side of his face into a single hard-twisted ringlet; short crisped whiskers, streaked with grey, encircle his face, and an imperial completes his hirsute attractions; his cheeks and forehead are marked with the small-pox.

He was attired in a grey and striped dress, the peculiarity of which was that the coat and vest were bound with wide stripes of black velvet. He speaks with but little of the peculiar negro dialect, except when he forgets himself for an instant, and unguardedly relapses into the old habits, which he has evidently carefully endeavored to overcome. He looked at his visitor very sharply for a minute or two, while he pretended to be abstractedly shuffling the cards; and collecting his valuable thoughts, at last he remarked:

"I s'pose you want me to run the cards for you?" The reply was in the affirmative, and the colored prophet concentrated his mind and began. Slowly he dealt the cards, and spake as follows:

"You don't believe in fortunes, my son—I see that. Must tell you what I see here—can't help it—if I see it in the cards, must tell you. You've had great deal trouble, my son; more comin'. Can't help it; mus' tell you. I see trouble in de cards; I see razackly what it is."

Here he suddenly stopped, and resuming his guarded manner, continued: "You've lost something, my son; something that you think a great deal of. Now I don't like to tell about lost things; I'se 'fraid I'll get myself into a snare; I'd rather not say nothing about it; fear I'll get myself into trouble." His auditor here gave him the most positive assurances that he should never be called into court to identify the thief of the missing article, and that he should be held free from all harm; whereupon he consented to impart the following information:

"Dis thing you lost is something that hangs up on a nail—something bright and round—you thinks a great deal of it, my son—when it went away it had on a bright guard—hasn't got a bright guard on now; got a black guard—you see I knows all about de article, my son, and I can tell you razackly where de article is—but

I'se rather not tell you 'bout it, my son; 'fraid I'll run myself into a snare; dat's the truth, my son, rather no say nothin' 'bout de article."

Being again assured of safety, he went on: "Well, my son, I'll tell you 'bout this yer thing. Has you got any boys in yer employ? No. Got two girls have you? One of dem girls is light-haired and de other is dark—the light one is de one who comes in your room in your boarding-house every morning when you'se gone away—'cause you lives in a boardin' house, I sees that—can see it in the cards, can always tell razackly. If you make a fuss about dat article you make your landlady feel bad. You has accused somebody of taking that article, but you 'cused de wrong person. The light-haired girl is who's got that article. Can't help it, my son, must tell you—de light-haired girl is de person. Mebbe she's put it back, my son, I'll see."

Here he cut the cards carefully, and continued:

"There's trouble 'bout dat article, my son, can't help it, must tell you—but you'll get the article, but you'll have disappointment. Whenever you see dat card you may know there's disappointment comin'—dat card is always disappointment—can't help it, my son, must tell you." Here he exhibited the nine of spades, to the malignant influence of which he attributed the future woes of his hearer.

"When you go home look in your bed between the mattresses and see if the article is there, for mebbe she'll put it back—if it aint there you must go to her and 'cuse her of it, 'cause it's in the house and she's got it—can't help it, my son, must tell you."

It is perhaps needless to say that the customer had met with no loss of property, and that all this was entirely gratuitous on the part of Mr. Grommer. Having, however, settled the matter to his satisfaction, that gentleman turned his attention to other things, and in the intervals of repeated shufflings and cuttings of the cards he said:

"Dere is a journey for you soon—and dis journey is going to be the best thing that ever happened to you—but dere is a little disappointment first—can't help it, my son, must tell—here you can see for yourself," and out came the malicious nine of spades again. "You will get money from beyond sea, my son—lots of money, lots of money, my son—here it is, you can see for yourself," and he exhibited the cheerful faces of the eight, nine, and ten of diamonds. "You will have disappointment before you get this money," and up came the hateful visage of the nine of spades once more. "You was born under a good star, my son—under a morning star—you was born under the planet Jupiter, my son, at 28 minutes past four in the morning—lucky star, my son, very lucky star. You are going to make a great change in your business, my son, which will be good; you will always be successful in business, but I think there is a little disappointment first; can't help it, must tell you." Here the listener looked for the nine of spades again, but it didn't come. "After a little while you turns your back on trouble; here, you can see for yourself—see, this is you."

The king of clubs was the Individual at that instant, and the troubles upon which he turned his back are, as nearly as he can remember, the knave of clubs, the nine of spades, and the deuce of diamonds.

The sage went on. "I'm comin' now to your marriage. You'se goin' to be married, but you'll have some disappointment first—can't help it, my son, must tell you. You see, here is a dark-complected lady that you like, and she has a heart for you, but her father don't like you—he prefers a young man of lighter complexion—see, here you all are, my son. This is you," and he showed the king of clubs—"and this is her." The "her" of whom he spoke so irreverently, was the queen of clubs. "This is the heart she has for you," and he exhibited the seven of that amorous suit. "This is her father"—the obstinate and cruel "parient" here displayed, was the king of spades—"and dis yer is de young man her father likes," and he placed before the eyes of the customer a hated rival in the shape of the knave of diamonds. "You see how it is, my son, dere is trouble between you—can't help it. You may possibly marry de dark-complected lady yet, but don't you do it, my son, don't you do it—now mind I tell you, don't you do it—she is not the lady for you—can't help it, must tell you; if you marry dat lady you will be sorry dat you ever tie de knot. See, here is the knot," and he showed the ace of diamonds. "See, this is the lady you ought to marry," and he produced the queen of diamonds; "and she will be your second wife if you do marry de dark-complected lady, but you'd better marry her first if you can get her, and let de dark-complected lady go for ebber; dat's so, my son, now mind I tell you."

He condescended no more, and the Cash Customer disbursed his dollar and departed, all the grandchildren gathering on the bank to give him three cheers as a parting salute.

CHAPTER XV.

How the "Individual" calls on Madame Clifton, of No. 185 Orchard Street, and how that amiable and gifted "Seventh daughter of a seventh daughter," prophesies his speedy death and destruction, together with all about the "Chinese Ruling Planet Charm."

CHAPTER XV.

MADAME CLIFTON, 185 ORCHARD STREET.

Perhaps there is no class of men brought constantly and prominently before the public eye, that is so great a puzzle to that public, as the class popularly denominated "sporting men." There is not a corner on Broadway where they do not congregate; there is not a theatre where they do not abound, and there is not a concert-room that does not overrun with them. There is a uniformity in their appearance that makes them easily recognised, for they all affect the ultra stylish in costume, even to the extreme of light kid gloves in the street; they all have the crisp moustache, the smooth-shaven cheeks, and the same keen, ever-watchful eye, constantly on the look-out for a "customer," that respectable word meaning, in their slang, a person to be victimized and swindled. Every lady who walks the street has to run the gauntlet of their insolent glances, and not unfrequently to hear their vulgar and offensive criticisms on her personal appearance; and every gentleman whose business calls him into Broadway of a pleasant day, has seen these persons grouped on the corner leisurely surveying the passers-by, or gathered into a little knot before some favorite rum-shop, discussing what is, to them, the absorbing topic of the day—probably the "good strike" Blobbsby made, "fighting the tiger," the night before; the "heavy run" a favorite billiard-player made on a certain occasion, or the respective chances of success of the two distinguished gentlemen who may chance at that time to be in training with a view of battering each other's heads until one concedes his claim to the brutal "honors" of the prize ring.

No gentlemen of fashion and fortune are more expensively dressed than these men; no class of people wear more finely stitched and embroidered linen, more costly broadcloth, more showy golden ornaments, or more brilliant diamonds; but for all, the man is yet to be found who has ever seen one of them put his hand or his brain to one single hour's honest work. Unsophisticated persons are often puzzled to account for the apparently irreconcilable circumstances of no work, and plenty of money, and in their endeavors to invent a plausible hypothesis on the basis of honesty, must ever be bewildered. The city man knows them at a glance to be "sporting men."

This phrase is a particularly comprehensive one; the "sporting man" is a gambler by profession, and therefore a swindler by necessity, for an "honest gambler" would fill a niche in the scale of created beings that has never yet been occupied; in addition to this, nearly every sporting man is a thief whenever opportunity offers. They probably would not pick a sober man's pocket, or knock him down at night and take his watch and money, for the risk of detection would be too great; but they are kept from downright stealing by no excess of virtue.

These remarks apply to the "sporting men," by profession—to those plausible gallows-birds who have no other ostensible means of getting a living. There are many men who sometimes spend an hour or two at a faro table, or who occasionally pass an evening in gambling at some other game, who do all fairly, and are above all suspicion of foul play; these persons are of course plundered by sharpers who surround them, and are called "good fellows" because they submit to their losses without grumbling.

The "sporting men" all have mistresses, on whom they sometimes rely for funds whenever an "unlucky hit," or a "bad streak of luck," has run their own purses low.

It is not part of the present purpose of this book to give particulars as to who and what their mistresses are, further than to state that at least one or two of the "Witches" described herein, officiate in that capacity. It is true, that the most of them are not of a style to tempt the lust of any man, but there are certain exceptions to the general rule, and in one or two instances the "Individual" found the fortune-teller to be comely and pleasant to the eye. As these women generally have plenty of money, they are very eligible partners for gamblers, who are liable to as many reverses as ever Mr. Micawber encountered, and who, when once down, might remain perpetually floored, did not some kind friend set them on their financial feet again.

And this is one of the duties of the monied mistress. When the "sporting man" is in funds, no one is more recklessly extravagant than he, and no one cuts a greater dash than his "ladye-love," if he chooses so to do; but when the cards run cross, and the purse is empty, it devolves upon her to furnish the capital to start in the world again.

The fact is well known to those who have taken the trouble to inquire into the subject, that several of the more fashionable fortune-tellers of the city sustain this sort of illicit relation to certain "sporting men," whose faces a man may see, perhaps, half a dozen times in the course of a lounge up and down Broadway of a pleasant afternoon.

Madame Clifton is, on the whole, a comely woman, and does a good business, but of course no sane person will think of applying these remarks personally to that respected matron.

The "Individual" paid a lengthened visit to Madame Clifton, and his remarks are recorded below. Because he met a sleek, close-shaved, finely moustached gentleman coming away from the door, he was of course not justified in believing that the said gentleman belonged to the establishment. Of course not.

The female professors of the black art hitherto visited by the Cash Customer, had not impressed him with a profound belief in their supernatural powers; he was "anxious," and was "awakened to inquiry," but he still had doubts, and there was great danger of his backsliding if there wasn't something immediately done for him.

He had been greatly disappointed by the absence from the domiciles of these good ladies of all the traditional necromantic implements and tools. His disposition to adhere to the modern witch-faith would have been greatly strengthened by the sight of a skull and cross-bones; a tame snake, or a little devil in a bottle, would have fixed his wavering belief; and his conversion would have been thoroughly assured by the timely exhibition of a broomstick on which he could see the saddle-marks.

None of these things had as yet been forthcoming, and the anxious inquirer, mourning the departure of all the romance of the art of witchcraft, was fast sinking into a state of incurable scepticism on the subject of even its utility, in the degenerate hands of modern practitioners. Hope had not, however, entirely deserted his heart, but still retained her fabled position in the bottom of his chest, near that important viscus, and he, therefore, courageously continued his pursuit of witchcraft under difficulties.

His next visit was to Orchard street, and he was induced to expect favorable results by the encouraging and positive assertion which concludes the subjoined advertisement, that "Madame Clifton is no humbug:"

"An Astrologist that beats the World, and $5,000 reward is offered to pay any person who can surpass her in giving correct statements on past, present, and future events, particularly absent friends, losses, lawsuits, &c. She also gives lucky numbers. She surpasses any person that has ever visited our city. She is also making great cures. All persons who are afflicted with consumption, liver complaint, scrofula, rheumatism, or any other lingering disease, would do well to call and see this wonderful and natural gifted lady, and you will not go away dissatisfied. N.B.—Madame Clifton is no humbug. Call and satisfy yourselves. Residence No. 185 Orchard-st., between Houston and Stanton."

Although Orchard Street is by no means so objectionable a thoroughfare as human ingenuity might make it, still, in spite of its pleasant-sounding name, it is not altogether a vernal paradise. If there ever was any fitness in the name it must have been many years ago, and the ancient orchard bears now no fruit, but low brick houses of assorted sizes and colors, seedy, and, in appearance, semi-respectable. Occasionally a blacksmith's shop, a paint room, or a livery stable, lower or meaner and more contracted than their neighbors, look as if they never got ripe, but had shrivelled and dropped off before their time.

The street is in a state of perennial bloom with half-built dwellings like gaudy scarlet blossoms, which are ripened into tenements by the fostering care of masons and carpenters with the most industrious forcing; and buds of buildings are scattered in every direction, in the shape of mortar-beds and piles of brick and lumber, waiting the due time for their architectural sprouting.

The house of Madame Clifton is of moderate growth, being but two stories high; it has a red brick front and green window-blinds, and is so ingeniously grafted to its nearest neighbor that some little care is necessary to determine which is the parent stock. It presents a fair outside, is but little damaged by age or weather, and is seemingly in a state of good repair.

A neat-looking colored girl answered the bell, and, showing our reporter into the parlor, asked his business, and if he "knew Madame Clifton's terms?"

Now when it is understood that fortune-telling is by no means the only, or the most lucrative part of Madame Clifton's business, it will be perceived that this inquiry had a peculiar significance. Having the fear of libel suits before his eyes, the Individual cannot state in precise and plain terms the exact nature of the business which the colored girl evidently thought had brought him there; he will content himself with delicately insinuating, that if his errand had been of the nature insinuated by that female delegate from Africa, there would have been a "lady in the case."

Fortunately the Cash Customer had erred not thus, but he made known to the colored lady his simple business.

Learning that he only wanted to have his fortune told by the Madame, and had no occasion to test her skill in the more expensive departments of her profession, the girl appeared to be satisfied of the responsibility of her visitor for that limited amount, and departed to inform her mistress.

The customer took an observation.

The room was a neatly-furnished parlor, a little flashy perhaps in the article of mirrors, but the sofas, chairs, carpet, &c., were plain and not offensive to good taste. A piano was in the room, but it was closed, and its tone and quality are unknown. One curious article, for a parlor ornament, stood in the corner of the room; it was the huge sign-board of a perfumery store, and bore in large letters the name of a dealer in sweet-scented merchandise, blazoned thereon in all the finery of Dutch metal and bronze. This conspicuous article, though mysterious and unaccountable, was not cabalistic, and savored not of witchcraft.

Presently the quiet colored girl returned, and in a low voice, and with a subdued well-trained manner, invited her visitor to follow her; meekly obeying, he was led up two flights of respectable stairs into a room wherein there was nothing mysterious, nor was there anything particularly suggestive except a large glass case filled with a stock of perfumery. What was the propriety of so very many bottles filled with perfumes and medicines did not at first appear; but the assortment of imprisoned odors, and liquid drugs, and the store-sign down stairs, and Madame Clifton, and a certain perfumery store in Broadway, and the proprietor thereof, so tangled themselves together in the brain of the inquirer that he has never since that time been able to disconnect one from the other.

Upon a small stand were two packs of cards—the one an ordinary playing pack, and the other what are known sometimes as fortune-telling cards. The devices on these latter differed materially from those in ordinary use; there were no plain cards; every one was ornamented with some kind of a significant design; there were pictures of women, of men, of ships and raging seas, of hearses, and sickbeds, and shrouds, and coffins, and corpses, and graves, and tombstones, and similar cheerful objects; then there were squares, and circles, and hands with scales, and hands with daggers, and hands sticking through clouds, and purses of money, and carriages, and moons, and suns, and serpents, and hearts, and Cupids, and eyes, and rays of light coming from nowhere, and shining on nothing, and Herculeses with big clubs, and big arms, bigger than the clubs, and big legs, bigger than both together, and swords, and spears, and sundials, and many other designs equally intelligible and portentous.

Soon the Madame appeared, and the attention of the Individual was immediately diverted from surrounding objects and riveted on the incomprehensible woman who was "no humbug," and who, according to her own opinion of herself, would have exactly realized Mr. Edmund Sparkler's idea of a "dem'd fine woman, with nobigodnonsense about her."

On the first glance, Madame Clifton is what would be called "fine-looking," but she does not analyse well. She is of medium height, aged about thirty-five years, with very light, piercing blue eyes, and very black hair, one little lock of which is precisely twisted into a very elaborate little curl, which rests in the middle of her forehead between her eyes, as if to keep those quarrelsome orbs apart. Her eyebrows are unusually heavy, so much so as to give a curious menacing look to the upper part of her face, which disagreeable expression is intensified by the extreme paleness of her countenance.

Her dress was unassuming, neat, and tasteful, save in the one article of jewelry, of which she wore as much as if the stock in trade at the Broadway perfumery store had been pearls, and gold, and diamonds, instead of perfumes and essences. Her deportment was self-possessed and lady-like, that is, if an expression of tireless watchfulness and unsleeping suspicion are consistent with refined and easy manners. She never took her steel-blue eyes from her visitor's face; she did not for an instant relax her confident smile; she did not speak but in the lowest softest tones; but her auditor felt every instant more convinced that the voice was the falsest voice he ever heard, the smile the falsest smile he ever saw, and that the cold piercing eye alone was true, and that was only true because no art could conceal its calculating glitter.

If one could imagine a smiling cat, Madame Clifton would resemble that cat more than any one thing in the world. Neat and precise in her outward appearance; not a fold of her garments, not a thread of lace or ribbon, not a hair of her head, but was exactly smooth and orderly, and in its exact place; not a glance of her eye that was not watchful and suspicious; not a tone or word that was not treacherous in sound; not a movement of body or of limb that was not soft and stealthy; her feline resemblances developed themselves more and more every instant, until at last the Individual came to regard her as some kind of dangerous animal in a state of temporary and perfidious repose. And this impression deepened every instant, so much so, that when the small soft hand was laid in his, he almost expected to see the sharp claws unsheathe themselves from the velvet finger-tips and fasten in his flesh.

The language she used, when freed from the technical phrases of her trade, was good enough for every day, and she did not distinguish herself by any specialty of bad English.

She asked her customer, with her most insinuating smile, if he would have her "run the cards for him," and on receiving an affirmative answer she took the pack of playing cards into her velvet hands, pawed them dexterously over a few times to shuffle them, laid them in three rows with the faces upward, and softly purred the following words:

"I am uncertain whether to run you a club or a diamond, for I do not exactly see how it is; but I will run you a club first, and if you find that it does not tell your past history, please to mention the fact to me, and I will then run you a diamond."

She then proceeded to mention a number of fictitious events which she asserted had happened in the past life of her listener, but that individual, who did not find that her revelations agreed with his own knowledge of his former history, tremblingly informed her of that fact; and she then, with a most vicious contraction of the overhanging eyebrows, broke short the thread of her fanciful story, and proceeded to "run him a diamond."

She evidently was determined to make the diamond come nearer the truth—to which end she dexterously strove by a series of very sharp cross-questionings to elicit some circumstance of his early history, on which she might enlarge, or to get some clue to his present circumstances, and hopes, and aspirations, that she might find some peg on which to hang a prediction with an appearance of probability. The Individual—with humiliation he confesses it—was a bachelor. His heart had proved unsusceptible, and Cupid had hitherto failed to hit him. On this occasion he proved characteristically unimpressible; and the insinuating smile, the inquiring look, and the winning manner, all failed of effect, and he remained pertinaciously non-committal.

Finding this to be the case, the feline Madame changed her tactics, and, as if to spite her intractable customer, began to prophesy innumerable ills and evils for him. She apparently strove to mitigate, in some degree, the sting of her predictions by an increased softness of manner, which was only a more cat-like demeanor than ever. She spoke as follows—the cold eye growing more cruel, and the wicked smile more treacherous every instant. First, however, came this guileful question, which was but a declaration of war under a flag of truce:

"You do not want me to flatter you, do you? You want me to tell you exactly what I see in the cards, do you not?" The customer stated that he was able to bear at least the recital of his future adversity, even if, when the reality came, he should be utterly smashed; whereupon she proceeded:

"I see here a great disappointment; you will be disappointed in business, and the disappointment will be very bitter and hard to bear—but that is not all, nor the worst, by any means. I see a burial—it may be only a death of one of your dearest friends, or some near relative, such as your sister, but I see that you yourself are weak in the chest and lungs; you are impulsive, proud, ambitious, and quick-tempered, which last quality tends much to aggravate any diseases of the chest, and I fear that the burial may be your own. Your disease is serious, you cannot live long, I think—I do not think you will live a year—in fact, there is the strongest probability that you will die before nine months. I think you will certainly die before nine months, but if you survive, it will only be after a most severe and painful illness, in the course of which you will undergo the extreme of human suffering. I see that you love a light-complexioned lady, but her friends object to her marriage with you, and are doing all they can to prevent it. A dark-complexioned man is trying to get her away from you; you must beware of him or he will do you great injury, for he has both the will and the power; he has already deceived and injured you, and will do so again even more deeply than he has yet. I see a journey, trouble, and misfortune, grief, sorrow, heavy loss, and heaviness of heart. I again tell you that you will die before nine months; but if you chance to survive, it will only be to encounter perpetual crosses and misfortunes. I might, if I was disposed to flatter you and give you false hopes, tell you that you will be lucky, fortunate in business, that you will get the lady, and I might promise you all sorts of good luck, but I don't want to flatter you; it would be much more agreeable to me to tell you a good life, for it sometimes pains me more than I can tell you to read bad lives to people, and I feel it very deeply; but I assure you that I never saw anybody's cards run as badly as do yours—I never saw so many losses and crosses, and so much trouble and misfortune in anybody's cards in my whole life—even if you outlive the nine months you will have the greatest trouble in getting the lady, and will always have bad luck."

She then tried by means of the cards to spell out the Inquirer's name, but failed utterly, not getting a single letter right; then she recommenced and threatened him with so much bad luck that he began almost to fear that he would break his leg before he rose from his chair, or would instantly fall down in a fit and be carried off to die at the Hospital. She told him that his lucky days were the 1st, 5th, 17th, 27th, and 29th of every month. Then perceiving that his feelings were deeply moved by the intractability of the "cruel parients" of the light-complexioned lady, and the black look of things generally, she slightly relented, and went on to say:

"If you will put your trust in me, and take my advice as a friend, I can sell you something that will surely secure you the lady, and thwart all your enemies—it is not for my interest that I tell you this, for upon my honor I make only five shillings upon fifty dollars' worth—it is no trick, but it is a charm which you must wear about you, and which you must wish over about the girl at stated times, and it will be sure to have the desired effect."

The customer asked the price of this wonderful charm.

"It is from five to fifty dollars, but as you are so extraordinarily unlucky I would advise you to take the full charm. It is the *Chinese Ruling Planet Charm*, and I import it from China at great expense. You must wear it about you, and every time you use it you must do it in the name of God; so you see there can be no demon about it. By means of this charm I have brought together husbands and wives who have been apart for three years, and I say a woman who can do that is doing good, and there is no demon about her. While you wear it you will not die or meet with bad luck, but it will change the whole current of your life."

She then told her unlucky hearer to make a wish and she would tell him by the cards whether he could have it or not. The answer was in the negative, and it was evident that nothing but the *Chinese Ruling Planet Charm* would save him, and no less than $50 worth of that. So the smiling Madame returned to the charge. "If you will take my advice as a friend, take the charm; it is for your sake only that I say this, for I make nothing by it—but I feel an interest in you, and I wish you would buy the charm for my sake as well as your own, for I want to see its effect on a fortune so bad as yours. If you don't buy it, and all kinds of ill-fortune befalls you, don't say I didn't warn you, and don't call Madame Clifton a humbug; but if you do buy it, you may be sure that you will ever bless the day you saw Madame Clifton."

It is, perhaps, needless to state that the Individual didn't have with him the fifty dollars to pay for the charm, but intimated that he would call again, after he got his year's salary.

She then said: "If you happen to call when I am engaged, tell the girl to say that you want to see me about *medicine*, and I will see you, for I never put off anybody who wants *medicine*, no matter who is with me, say *medicine*, and I will see you instantly." Here she softly showed her visitor to the door, and smiled on him until he stood on the outside steps. He then departed, secretly wondering what kind of "medicine" she was prepared to furnish in case any unlooked for occasion should suggest a second call. Her last remark suggested that Madame Clifton derives a larger profit from the peculiar kinds of "*medicine*" she deals in, than from all her other witchery.

CHAPTER XVI.

Details the particulars of a morning call on Madame Harris, of No. 80 West 19th Street, and how she covered up her beautiful head in a black bag.

CHAPTER XVI.

MADAME HARRIS, No. 80 WEST 19th STREET, NEAR SIXTH AVENUE.

Madame Harris is one of the most ignorant and filthy of all the witches of New York. She does not depend entirely on her "astrology" for her subsistence, but relies on it merely to bring in a few dollars in the spare hours not occupied in the practice of the other dirty trades by which she picks up a dishonest living. She has a good many customers, and in one way and another she contrives to get a good deal of money from the gullible public. She has been engaged in business a number of years, and has thriven much better than she probably would, had she been employed in an honester avocation.

The "Individual" paid her a visit, and carefully noted down all her valuable communications; he has told the whole story in the words following:

We all believe in Aladdin, and have as much faith in his uncle as in our own; but we don't know the pattern of his lamp, we have no photograph of the genii that obeyed it, and we can make no correct computation of the market value of the two hundred slaves with jars of jewels on their heads. The customer, who is determined that posterity shall be able to make no such complaint of him or of his history, here solemnly undertakes, upon the faith of his salary, to relate the unadorned truth, and to indulge in no *ad libitum* variations—imagining, while he writes, that he sees in the distance the critical public, like a many-headed Gradgrind, singing out lustily for "Facts, sir, facts."

The next fact, then, to be investigated and sworn to, is this Madame Harris, a very dirty female fact indeed, residing in the upper part of the city, and advertising as follows:

"Madame Harris.—This mysterious Lady is a wonder to all—her predictions are so true. She can tell all the events of life. Office, No. 80 West 19th-st., near 6th-av. Hours 10 a.m. to 6 p.m. Ladies 25 cts.; Gentlemen 50 cts. She causes speedy marriages; charge extra."

Wearily the inquirer plodded his way on foot to West 19th Street, fearing to trust himself to a stage or car, lest the careless conversation of the unthinking, and the reprehensible jocularity of the little boys who hang about the corners of the streets which intersect the Sixth Avenue, and pelt unwary passengers with paving-stones, should divert his mind from the importance and great moral responsibility of his mission.

After encountering a large assortment of the dangers and discomforts incident to pedestrianism in New York in muddy weather, he achieved West 19th street, and stood in sight of the mysterious domicile of Madame Harris.

It is a tenement house, shabby-genteel even in its first pretentious newness; but it has now lost its former appearance even of semi-respectability, and has degenerated to a state of dirt only conceivable by those unhappy families who live two in a house, and are in a constant state of pot-and-kettle war, and of mutual refusing to clean out the common hall.

A little mountain of potato skins, and bones, and other kitchen refuse, round which he was forced to make a detour, plainly said to the traveller that the population of the house No. 80 were in the habit of depositing garbage in the gutters, under cover of the night, and in violation of the city ordinance. A highly-perfumed atmosphere surrounds this delightful abode, for the first floor thereof is occupied as a livery stable, which constantly exhales those sweet and pungent odors peculiar to equine habitations.

Pulling the sticky bell-handle with as dainty a touch as possible, the Individual was admitted by a slatternly weak-eyed girl of about eighteen, with her hair and dress as tumbled as though she had just been run through a corn-shelling machine, and who was so unnecessarily dirty that even her face had not been washed. She was further distinguished by a wart on her nose of such shape and dimensions that it gave her face the appearance of being fortified by a many-sided fort, which commanded the whole countenance.

This interesting young female welcomed her visitor with a clammy "Come in," and led the way up stairs, he following, in due dread of being for ever extinguished by an avalanche of unwashed keelers and kettles, which were unsteadily piled up on the landing, and which an incautious touch would have toppled over, and deluged the stairs with unknown sweet-smelling compounds, whose legitimate destination was the sewer. On the second floor, directly, judging from the noise, over the stall of the balkiest horse in the stable below, is the room of the Madame.

The customer took an observation:

The furnishings of the apartment showed an attempt to keep up a show, which was by far too miserably transparent to hide the slovenliness which peeped out everywhere through the tawdry gilding. There were so many oil paintings on the walls, in such gaudy frames, that it seemed as if the room had been dipped into a bath of cheap auction pictures, and hadn't been wiped dry, or had been out in a shower of them, and hadn't come in until it had got very wet. A broad gilt window cornice stood leaning in the corner of the room, instead of being in its legitimate place; a pair of lace curtains were wadded up and thrown in a chair, while the windows were covered with the commonest painted muslin shades; a piano-stool stood in the middle of the room, but there was no piano.

These were the indications of "better days;" these were the shallow traps set to inveigle the beholder into a belief in the opulence of the occupants of this charming residence.

But the little cooking-stove, on which two smoothing irons were heating, the scraps of different patterned carpets which hid the floor, and made it appear as if covered with some kind of variegated woollen chowder, the second-hand, conciliating please-buy-me look of the three chairs, and the dirt and greasy grime which gave a character to the place, told at once the true state of facts.

On one side of the room was a little door, evidently communicating with a closet or small bedroom; on this door was a slip of tin, on which was painted

Office.—Madam Harris, Astrologist.

and into this "office" the weak-eyed girl disappeared, with a shame-faced look, as if she had tried to steal her visitor's pocket-book, and hadn't succeeded. Presently there came from the closet a sound of half-suppressed merriment, as if a constant succession of laughs were born there, full grown and boisterous, but were instantly garroted by some unknown power, until each one expired in a kind of choky giggle. There was also a noise of the making of a bed, the hustling of chairs, the putting away of toilet articles out of sight, and over all was heard the chiding voice of Madame Harris, who was evidently dressing herself, superintending these other various operations, and scolding the weak-eyed maiden all at once.

At last this latter individual got so far the better of her jocularity that she was able to deport herself with outward seriousness when she emerged from the mysterious closet, and said to the Individual, "Walk in." At this time she was under so great a head of laugh that she would inevitably have exploded, had she not, the instant her visitor turned his back, let go her safety-valve, and relieved herself by a guffaw which would have been an honor and a credit to any one of the horses on the first floor.

The room in which Madame Harris was waiting to receive her customer was so dark that he stumbled over a chair, and fell across a bed before he could see where he was. Then he recovered himself, and took an observation.

The room was a very small one—so diminutive, indeed, that the bed, which occupied one side of it, reduced the available space more than two-thirds. It was partitioned off from the rest of the room by a dirty patch-work bed-quilt, with more holes than patches. The walls were scrawled over with pencil-marks, evidently drawings made by young children, who had the usual childish notions of proportion and perspective; and on one side of the wall, near the head of the bed, a bit of pasteboard persisted in this startling announcement—

tERms CasH

A narrow strip of rag carpet was on the floor; a small stand and a chair completed the furnishing of the room, and a single smoky pewter lamp exhausted itself in a dismal combat with the gloom, which constantly got the better of it.

When the Cash Inquirer stumbled, and took an involuntary leap into the middle of the bed, an awful voice came out of the dreariness, saying, "There is a chair right there behind you." This information proved to be correct, and the discomfited delegate subsided into it, and gazed stolidly at the Madame. If Madame Harris were worth as much by the pound as beef, her market-price would be about twenty-five dollars. She was attired in a loose morning-gown, of an exceedingly flashy pattern, open before, disclosing a skirt meant to be white, but whose cleanliness was merely traditional. Of her countenance her visitor cannot speak, for it was carefully hidden from his inquiring gaze, and its unknown beauties are left to the imagination of the reader. Perched mysteriously on the back of her head, where it was retained by some feminine hocus-pocus, which has ever been a sealed mystery to *man*kind, was a little black bonnet, marvellous in pattern and design; from this depended a long black veil, covering her countenance, and disguising her as effectually as if she had washed her face and put on a clean dress.

She proceeded at once to business, and opened conversation with this appropriate remark: "My terms is fifty cents for gentlemen, and the pay is always in advance."

Here followed a disbursement on the part of the anxious seeker after knowledge, and an approving chuckle was heard under the veil.

Taking up a pack of cards so overlaid with dirt that it was a work of time and study to tell a queen from a nine spot, or distinguish the knaves from the aces, she presented them with the imperative remark: "Cut them once."

Then ensued the following wonderful predictions uttered by a dubious and uncertain voice under the veil—which voice seemed one minute to come from the mouth, then it issued from the throat, then it sprawled out of the stomach, then it was heard from the back of the head under the bonnet, and in the course of a few minutes it came from so many places, that the puzzled hearer was dubious as to its exact whereabouts—these curious effects being, doubtless, attributable to the thick covering over the face. But its various communications, when gathered together, were found to sum up as follows:

"You face back misfortune and trouble, of which you have had much, but they are now behind you, and you have no more to fear. You will henceforth be successful in business, you will have a great deal of money. Your affection card faces up a young woman with dark eyes and dark hair, about twenty-three years old; she is older than she has led you to believe; there is a dark-complexioned man whom you will see in two days, who is your enemy; you may not know it, but you had better beware of him, for he will do you an injury, if he can; you will see him and speak with him the night of day-after-to-morrow. Your marriage card faces up this dark woman, as I said before. I don't see a great deal of money layin' round her, but there is plenty of money layin' round you in the future. Somebody will die and leave you money within nine weeks, not counting this week. You was born under the planet Mars, which gives you two lucky days in every week—Mondays and Thursdays; anything you begin on those days will surely succeed."

Here she handed the cards to be cut again, which operation disclosed a new feature in the Individual's matrimonial future, for she went on to say:

"There is another woman who faces your love-card, who has light hair and light eyes; she favors your love-card and will be your first wife; you will have five children—four girls and one boy; look out for the dark-complexioned man, for he favors your first wife, and, though she does not favor him very much, he will try to get her away from you. Your line of life is long; you will live to be sixty-eight years old, but you will die very suddenly, for your line of death crosses your line of life very suddenly, which always brings sudden death."

Having given this cheering promise, she again held out the cards to be cut, and said, "Cut them again now, and make a wish at the same time, and I will tell you if you will have your wish."

When the required ceremony had been solemnly performed, she continued: "You will have your wish, but not right away; don't expect to get it before week after next, but then you will be sure to have it, for there is no disappointment in the cards for you." She then informed her customer that she always answered unerringly two questions, which he was now at liberty to propound. He made a couple of inquiries relative to his future business prospects, and received in reply the promise of most gratifying results.

Having then, as he supposed, got his money's worth, he was about to take his leave, when she interrupted him thus:

"I have a charm for securing good luck to whoever wears it; you can wear it, and your most intimate friend would never suspect it; my charge is one dollar for gentlemen; a great many have bought it of me; many merchants who were on the point of failing have come to me and possessed this charm, and been saved; you had better possess it, for it will be sure to bring you good luck; if you possess it, you will always be successful in business; Mr. Lynch of Mott Street possessed it, and has been very lucky ever since, besides a great number I could name; my advice to you is, possess the charm."

She then put her elbows on her knees after the manner of a Fulton Market apple-pedler, in which classic attitude she awaited an answer. The decision was not favorable to her hopes; for the economical customer concluded not to invest in the charm, although it had brought such excellent fortune to Mr. Lynch of Mott Street. He departed, encountering again in his progress the weak-eyed one, who met him with a smile, escorted him to the door with a great laugh, and dismissed him with a joyous grin.

CHAPTER XVII.

Treats of the peculiarities of several
Witches in a single batch.

CHAPTER XVII.

A BATCH OF WITCHES.

The fortune-tellers so elaborately described in the foregoing chapters are by no means the only ones in New York, engaged in that lucrative occupation; there are several others who were visited by the Individual, but who in their surroundings approach so nearly to those already set down, that a detailed description of each would necessarily be a somewhat monotonous repetition. So the prophecy only of each one is here writ down, with a few words suggestive of the character of the immediate neighborhood, leaving the imaginative reader to fill up the blank himself, or to turn back to some foregoing chapter for a picture of a similar locality, if he prefers it ready-made to his hands.

MADAME DE BELLINI,
No. 159 FORSYTH STREET.

For the benefit of those not familiar with the streets of New York, it is perhaps well to mention that Forsyth Street is a dirty thoroughfare, two streets east of the Bowery, and that it is filled for the most part with small groceries, junk shops, swill milk dispensaries, and stalls for the sale of diseased vegetables and decaying fruit, and that the inhabitants are mostly delegates from Africa, and from the Green Isle of the Sea.

Immediately adjoining the domicil of Madame de Bellini is a filthy little vegetable store, and on the opposite corner is an equally filthy Irish grocery, where are dispensed swill milk and poisoned whiskey. The residence of the Madame is a low two-story brick house, of rather better appearance than many of its neighbors, which are principally wooden buildings with those old-fashioned peculiar roofs, with little windows close under the cornice, which make a house look as if it had had its hat knocked over its eyes.

Madame de Bellini is a Dutchwoman of very large dimensions, being a two-hundred-and-fifty-pounder at the lowest estimate. Like most fat women, she is good-natured and smiling. She is apparently 35 years old, of pleasant manners, somewhat embarrassed by the difficulty she has in communicating her ideas in English, and is much neater in person and dress than the majority of ladies in the same line of business. She would be a popular bar-maid at a lager-bier saloon, and would preside over the fortunes of the sausage and Swiss cheese table, with eminent success, and satisfaction to the public.

She welcomed the Cash Customer in a jolly sort of way, introduced him to her private apartment, and seated him on a chair at one side of a little table, while she bestowed herself on a stool opposite.

Having ascertained that he did not speak German with sufficient fluency to carry on an animated conversation in that tongue, or to comprehend a rapidly spoken discourse delivered therein, she was compelled to ventilate her English, which she did, beginning as follows:

"I speak not vera mooch goot English—I speak German and French, but no goot English."

The Individual, with his usual caution, inquired how much she proposed to charge for her services. She responded thus:

"I tell your for*toon* fier ein tollar, or I can tell your for*toon* fier ein half-tollar."

Fifty cents' worth was enough to begin with, so she took his left hand in her huge fist, and as a preliminary operation squeezed it till he gave it up for lost, and in the intervals of his suffering hastily ran over in his mind the various ways in which one-handed people get a living; then she relented and did not deprive him of that useful member, but said:

"You have goot hand, vera goot hand—your hand gifs you goot fortoon. You was born under goot blanet, vera nice blanet, you have vera nice fortoon. You have mooch rich, vera great monish; you haf seen drubbles, (trouble) vera mooch drubbles—more drubbles you haf seen, as you will see some more—dat is, you shall not have so many drubbles py and py as you haf had long ago, for you haf goot blanet. You will journeys make mooch in footoor (future) years. You will have two wifes and mooch kindes (children) in der footoor years, and you will be vera mooch happy und bleasant mit der wife vot you shall have der first dime, but not so mooch happy und bleasant mit der wife vot you shall have der two time, but you shall vera mooch monish have in der fortoor years."

She then released the hand of her visitor, who was very glad to get it back again, and took up a pack of cards, which she manipulated in the customary style, and then said:

"Your carts run vera nice; you have goot carts; here is a shentleman's as ish vera goot to you, he is great friends mit you: here is a letter vot you shall be come to you right avays vera soon—it ish goot news to you; you must do joost vot das letter says. Here ish a brown girls vot lofs (loves) you vera mooch, but you do not lofs dat girls, so much as das girls lofs you—you will not be der vife of das girl, for there is anunther girls vot you lofs bretty bad und you will marry her; she is bretty goot girls und you will be happy, you will hof lots of kindes mit das girls. Das girls haf a man now vos lof her vera mooch—he is was you call das soldier; he lofs her mooch but he shall not hof her, you shall hof das girls. Here is great man was will be good friend to you; he ish vera great man, a big king; not vas you call der könig, but your big mans, your, vos is das, your bresident—de bresident bees goot friends mit you—here is dark mans, he ish no goot friend mit you, und you must keep away from das dark mans."

This was all the information she appeared to derive from this pack, which were ordinary playing cards, so she laid them aside and took up the regular fortune-telling cards, which are covered with various mysterious devices. These did not seem to communicate anything of very special importance in addition to what she had already said, for she examined them closely and then merely summed up as follows:

"Goot fortoon, goot blanet, goot vifes, blenty monish, mooch kindes, not more troubles in der footoor years, big friends, bresident mooch friends mit you, lif long, ninety-nine years before you die, leave fortoon to vife und two kindes."

The Individual was curious to inquire wherein the fifty-cent dose he had received, differed from the fortunes for which she charged "ein tollar," and he received the following information:

"For ein tollar I gifs you a charm as you vears on your necks, und it gifs you goot luck for ever, und you never gets drownded, und you lifs long viles, und you bees rich und vera mooch happy."

The Madame was also good-natured enough to exhibit one of these powerful charms to her customer. It was a piece of parchment, originally about four inches square, but which had been scalloped on the edges, and otherwise cut and carved; on it were inscribed in German, several cabalistic words; this potent document was to be always worn next the heart.

Madame de Bellini has been in New York but a year or two; she speaks French and German, and is taking lessons in English from an American lady. She has many customers, mostly German, and, as in the case of all the other witches, the greatest majority of her visitors are women.

MADAME LEBOND, No. 175 HUDSON STREET.

The house in which this woman was sojourning at the time of the visit hereinafter described, is a boarding-house, and the room of the Madame is the back parlor on the second floor.

The Individual was received at the door by a short, greasy, dirty man, about forty years of age, who invited him into the front parlor, to wait until the Madame was disengaged. This man, who is an ignorant, half-imbecile person, passes for the husband of the fortune teller, and is known as *Doctor* Lebond. He is a man of peculiar appearance; the top of his head is perfectly bald, and the fringe of hair about the lower part of it, is twisted into long corkscrew ringlets, that fall low down on his shoulders.

He informed the customer that the Madame was then engaged, but he seemed undecided about the exact nature of her present employment. He first said she was "tellin' the futur for a young gal;" then she was "engaged with a literary man;" then "a dry-goods merchant wanted to find out if his head clerk didn't drink;" but finally he said that "Madame L. is a eatin' of her dinner." After some ingenious drawing-out, the *Doctor* vouchsafed the subjoined statement of his business prospects.

"We seen the time when we hadn't fifteen minutes a day, on account of young gals a comin' for to have their fortune told; we used to be busy from mornin' till ten and 'levin o'clock at night a-tellin' fortunes an' a doctorin'—but now, we don't do so much 'cause the young gals don't like to come to a boardin'-house where young men can see 'em, 'specially in the evenin'. We's too public here; the young men a-boardin' here likes for to have the young gals come, they likes for to see 'em in the parlor, but the young gals won't come so much, 'cause we's too public. We'll have for to get another house on account of business.

"I don't get so much doctorin' to do as I used to, 'cause we's too public. I have doctored lots of folks, principally young fellers and young gals, and I can do it right. If you ever get into any trouble you'll find me and my wife *all right*; you can come to us—we mean to be all right, and to give everybody the worth of their money, and we *is* all right."

By this time, Madame Lebond had finished her dinner, and was waiting in the back parlor. She is a fat, slovenly-looking woman, forty years old or more, having no teeth, and taking prodigious quantities of snuff, which gives her enunciation some peculiar characteristics.

When the Individual first beheld her, she was standing in the middle of the floor, picking her teeth. She requested her visitor to take a seat, and to pay her half-a-dollar, with both of which requests he complied. She then put into his hand the end of a brass tube about an inch in diameter and a foot long, and said: "Give be the tibe of your birth as dear as possible."

This was done, and the following brief dialogue ensued:—

"Was you bord id the bording?"

"I really don't remember."

"Do you have beddy dreabs?"

"I do not dream much."

"Thed you dod't have bad dreabs?"

"No."

"Thed you was bord id the bording," by which mysterious word she probably meant, "morning." She then continued:—

"You are a pretty keed sbart chap—sharp id busidess, but dot good id speculatiods, ad you should codfide your attedtiods to busidess. If you keep od as you are goidg dow, ad works hard, ad dod't bix id bad cobpady, ad is hodest, ad dod't spend your buddy, you will be rich. You will travel buch—you *have* travelled buch, but your travels is hardly begud; there is a lodg jourdey at sea dow before you, ad you will start od this jourdey bost udexpectedly; you will always be lucky, ad will be very rich. I dod't say dothin' to flatter do wud; lots of fellers ad gals cub here ad I tell theb all jest what I see; if I see bad luck I tell theb so; but yours is all good luck, ad I see lots of it for you. You have had bad luck lately, but you will get over your bad luck for you are a pretty sbardt chap, ad have got a good deal of abbitiod, ad you go ahead pretty well. You will barry a gal—a gal as you have seed but dod't know. Very well, she is a youdg gal, ad a rich gal, ad a good-lookidg gal; you will dot barry her for sobe tibe, but you will barry her at last. She has a beau ad you will likely have sobe trouble with hib, but you will get the gal at last. The gal has light hair ad blue eyes, ad I cad show her to you if you would like to see her."

Of course the visitor liked to see her; so he was directed to clasp the brass tube in his right hand, and place his hand over the top. Then she stepped behind his chair and began to go through with some extraordinary manual exercises on his head. She felt of the bumps, she squeezed his head, punched it, jerked it from side to side, and twisted it about in every possible direction. What was the object and intention of this performance she did not disclose, but when she had kneaded his unfortunate skull to her satisfaction, she bade him step to the window and look into the tube.

This he did, and he saw a very dingy-looking daguerreotype of a fair-haired damsel with blue eyes, who bore, of course, not the most distant resemblance to any lady of his acquaintance.

Then the fat Madame had a charm to sell, to be worn about the neck, and never taken off, in which case it would secure for the wearer "good luck" for ever.

The Individual declined to purchase and departed, meeting at the door the curly *Doctor*, who once again offered his medical services in case the stranger ever got into "trouble," and who once again assured that person with an air of mystery that "me and my wife is all right—yes, you may depend, we is all right, we is."

MADAME MAR, AND MADAME DE GORE, No. 176 VARICK STREET.

These two eminent sorceresses are in partnership, and drive a tolerably fair trade. They advertise in the papers, one week the heading being "Madame Mar, assisted by Madame de Gore," and the next week, it will be "Madame de Gore, assisted by Madame Mar," and the profits of the business are shared in the same impartial manner.

The house, No. 176, is in the worst part of Varick Street, and the room occupied by the pair of witches is over a boot and shoe store, and a pawnbroker's shop is directly opposite.

The room is a small parlor, neatly though plainly furnished, and with no professional implements visible. When the inquirer made his call, Madame de Gore was engaged in the kitchen, in her various household duties, and Madame Mar attended to his call. She is a tall and rather pleasing woman, neatly dressed and of quiet manners.

She secured a dollar in advance, and then led her customer into a little closet-like room, furnished only with a small table and two chairs. She then announced that she is a "phrenologist," and exhibited a plaster bust with the "bumps" scientifically marked out, and also some phrenological charts and other publications. She proceeded to give the character of her visitor in the usual mode of phrenological examinations, after which she prophesied as follows:

"You were born between Jupiter and Mars, with such stars you can never be unlucky, for although you have seen trouble, it is past. Your luck runs in threes and fives—that is, you are unlucky three years in succession, and lucky the five years following. You are never *very* unlucky, but you do not do so well in your third house as in your fifth house. You could not be unlucky in your fifth house if you tried. You have now two months to run in your third house, then comes on your fifth house. Just now your life seems to be under a cloud, but after two months you will come out bright and will enjoy five years of clear sunshine, and you will then be very wealthy. You will have more money then than you ever will again, though you will always have plenty. Your wealth runs 14 at the end of five years; after that runs 13½, which is very wealthy. You will marry a young girl, wealthy and beautiful. You will raise two daughters, but you will never have a large family. You will be the father of many children, but your family will never be more than two children. You will go in business with a very wealthy Southern man, his wealth runs 14—he has two sons and a daughter. You will marry the daughter, though you will be opposed by the father and one son, but the other son will stick by you. You will live with that wife twenty-five years, then she will die and you will travel with your two daughters. You will go to Europe. In England you will marry a French widow. Your two daughters will marry well, and at 72 or 73 years old you will die, leaving a widow, two daughters, and a large fortune."

Madame de Gore did not make her appearance at all, and after Madame Mar had failed to induce her visitor to pay her an extra dollar for a phrenological chart, she politely showed him out.

MADAME LANE, No. 159 MULBERRY STREET.

This distinguished lady lives in a dirty, dilapidated mansion, at the corner of Grand and Mulberry Streets. The Cash Customer was admitted by the Madame herself, who desired him to be seated for a few minutes, until she had concluded her business with a boy of about 17 years old, who had called to find out what would be the winning numbers in the next Georgia lottery. Two dirty-faced children were playing about the room, making a great noise.

One corner of the room was fenced off with rough boards, forming a narrow closet, in which two people could, with some difficulty, sit down. This was the astrological chamber; the mystic room into which visitors were conducted to have their fortunes told.

Madame Lane is of the Irish breed; is red-haired, freckled, and dirty to a degree. Her dress was ragged, showing a soiled, dingy petticoat through the rents.

She seated her customer in the little room, produced a pack of cards, and proceeded to tell his future, at times shouting out threats and words of warning to the noisy brats outside. Then she said:

"You are a man as has seen a great deal of trouble in the past."

It will be noticed that this is almost a universal remark with the witches, probably because it is a perfectly safe thing to assert of any person in the world.

"Yes, you have seen trouble in the past, not *real* trouble, such as sickness, or losses in business, but still, trouble, and your mind has been going this way and that way and t'other way, but now all your trouble and disappointment is past, and your mind won't go this way and that way any more. Stop that noise you brats or I'll beat you." (This to the children.)

"Your cards run lucky, 'cause you were born under Jupiter, and folks as is borned under Jupiter will always be lucky in business, in love, and in everything they undertake. If your business sometimes goes this way, and that way, and t'other way, it will all come out right, for when a man is borned under Jupiter he must be all right in his business, and in his love, and in his marriage, and in his children. Young ones stop that noise or I'll beat you black and blue. You have had sickness lately and your mind has been going this way, and that way, and t'other way, but you need not worry for it will be all right soon. Children stop that row or clear right out to the kitchen. Now mind. I tell you. I see a girl here that loves you very much, but you don't love her and won't marry her, but you will marry another girl with black whiskers; no, I mean the feller that is coortin' her has got black whiskers, and I fear you will have trouble with black whiskers if you are not careful—the girl has got black hair and is miserable because you don't write to her. I'm coming after you, young ones there, with a raw hide and I'll cut the skin off your backs. You will marry this gal and you will be very happy, and will have three children, which will be joys to you. Children, I'll come and kill you in two minutes. And you will always be prosperous in your business, and you will be very rich, and you will live to be eighty-five years old. Now you can cut the cards and make a wish and I will tell you if it will come true. Yes, your wish will come true, because you have cut the knave, and queen, and king—if you'd like a speedy marriage with the gal I told you of, I'll fix it for you for fifty cents extra; children if you don't shut up I'll come and beat you blind."

The Individual invested a half-dollar as requested, and received in return a white powder with these instructions;—

"You will burn that powder just before you get into bed, and if you see the gal to-night you won't see no change in her, but she will be changed to-morrow. She is kinder down on you now, but she loves you though her mind is kinder this way and that way, but she will be changed toward you to-night by what I will do after you are gone."

The customer departed, leaving this fond mother engaged in an active skirmish with the two children, both of whom finally escaped into the street with great howlings.

Madame Lane does a good business. She says that in pleasant weather she has from twenty-five to fifty calls a-day, mostly women; but in bad weather not more than fifteen or twenty, and these of the other sex. Many of these come only to learn lucky numbers for lottery gambling, and policy playing.

CHAPTER XVIII.

CONCLUSION.

It has been already mentioned that there are a number of persons in the city who do more or less in the fortune-telling way, who never advertise for customers. These we must leave to their own seclusion; as our business has been with those who make a business of this species of swindling, and who use all manner of arts to entice the curious, or the credulous, into their dens, there not only robbing them of their money, but often putting them in the way to be injured much more deeply. This, of course, is especially the case with young girls.

In order to give the readers of this book an idea of the part taken by these fortune-telling women in many of the terrible dramas of crime constantly enacting in city life, an extract showing the *modus operandi* is here inserted. It is from one of a series of very useful little books published in this city, and entitled, "Tricks and Traps of New York."

Speaking of New York fortune-tellers, the author says, having previously indulged in some severe remarks about "yellow-covered" novels:

"To see how the fortune-teller performs her part, let us suppose a case:

"A young, credulous girl, whose mind has been poisoned by the class of fictions above referred to, is induced to visit a modern witch, for the purpose of having her 'fortune told.' The woman is very shrewd, and perceives, in a moment, the kind of customer she has to deal with. Understanding her business well, she is perfectly aware that love and marriage—courtship, lovers, and wedded bliss—are the subjects which are most agreeable.

"She begins by complimenting her customer: 'such beautiful eyes, such elegant hair, such a charming form, and graceful manners, are altogether too fine for a servant or working girl.' She must surely be intended for a higher station in life, and she will certainly attain it. She will rise in the world, by marriage, and will one day be one of the finest ladies in the land. Her husband will be the handsomest man she has ever seen, and her children will be the most beautiful in the world. Fortune-tellers always foretell many children to their female customers; for the instinct of maternity, the yearning desire for offspring, is one of the strongest feelings of human nature.

"Much more of this sort is said; and if the witch finds her talk eagerly listened to, she knows exactly how to proceed. She appoints days for other visits; for she desires to get as many half-dollars out of her dupe as she can. Meantime, the girl has been thinking of what she has heard, has pictured to herself a brilliant future—a rich husband—every luxury and enjoyment—and, upon the whole, has built so many castles in the air, that her brain is half-bewildered. Even though she may not believe a tittle of what is said to her, feminine curiosity will generally lead her to make a second visit; and when the fortune-teller sees her come upon a like errand a second time, she sets down her prey as tolerably sure and lays her plans accordingly.

"She goes on to state to the girl, in her usual rigmarole style, that she will, in a few weeks, meet with a lover; and perhaps she may receive a present of jewelry; and by that she will know that the 'handsome young man' has seen, and been smitten by her many charms.

"When the half-believing girl has gone, the scheming sorceress calls to her aid her confederate in the game—the party who is to personate 'the handsome young man.' This is usually a spruce-looking fellow, who makes this particular kind of work his regular business; or it may be some rich debauchee, who is seeking another victim, will come and lie in wait, either behind the curtain or in the next room, where, through some well-contrived crevice, he can see and hear all that is going on. One or the other of these men it is that is to assist the witch in fulfilling her prophecies; who is, at the proper time, to be in the way to personate the 'young beau,' or 'rich southerner,' and to induce her to visit a house of assignation, or, in some way, accomplish her ruin.

"Persons who have been puzzled to know how many of the young fellows get their living who are seen about town, always well dressed, and with plenty of cash, and yet having no apparently respectable means of living, will find a future solution of their questions in this explanation. Many of these men are 'kept' by their mistresses, or by the proprietors of houses of ill-fame; in the latter case, to make acquaintance with strangers, and to bring business to those houses. They are often very fine-looking and well-appearing men, and possessed of good natural abilities; but, from laziness or crime, or some other cause, adopt the meanest possible business a man can stoop to. Humiliating as this may seem, and degrading as it is to poor human nature, what we state is, nevertheless, the literal truth.

"But, to come back to our supposed case. A few days after her visit to the witch, the girl actually does, perhaps, receive a present, as the witch predicted; this not only pleases her vanity and love of admiration, but disposes her to put confidence in the powers of the fortune-teller to read coming events. Straightway the deluded girl goes again to the witch, to tell how things have fallen out, as she foretold, and to seek further light upon the subject. It is now the cue of the prophetess to describe the young man. This she does in glowing terms; never failing to endow him with a large fortune; and the poor girl goes away with her head more turned than ever."

"Enraptured with a description, or sight of the picture of her fond love, the deluded girl is now all anxiety to see him in person. The witch accordingly gives her some magical powder (price one dollar), which she is to put under her pillow every night for seven nights, or wear next her heart for nine days, or some other nonsense of that kind, at the end of which time, she is told to take the ferry-boat to Hoboken or some such place, at a certain hour in the afternoon, and somewhere on her route she will have a sight of the gentleman she is almost crazed to see. The result is plain, the 'gentleman' is there as foretold, an acquaintance is commenced, and the girl is ultimately ruined.

"We have been thus particular to give, step by step, the details of the mode of management pursued in these cases. There are, of course, many varieties, dictated by the circumstances of each case, but the general features and the *result*, are the same.

"The incidents above given are the outlines of a real case in which the end of the conspirators was accomplished; the girl, however, was rescued by the Managers of the Magdalen Asylum, and is now leading a blameless life."

The "Individual" has now concluded his labors, and he hopes not without profit to the community at large.

He has heard it urged that this book will merely advertise the fortune-tellers, and that they will go on driving a more flourishing trade than ever. He cannot think that this will be the case; he cannot believe that any persons who read in this book the candid exposition of the style of necromancy dealt out by the modern Circes, will be willing to pay money for any personal experience of them, and he respectfully submits that although they have heretofore been consulted by many ladies of respectability, from motives of mere curiosity, those ladies will risk no further visits when they learn that they may with as much propriety visit any other assignation house, as a fortune-teller's den.

A recapitulation of the various prophecies made to the Cash Customer would show that he has been promised thirty-three wives, and something over ninety children—that he was brought into the world on various occasions between 1820 and 1833—that he was born under nearly all the planets known to astronomers—that he has more birth-places than he has fingers and toes—that he has passed through so many scenes of unexpected happiness and complicated misfortune in his past life, that he must have lived fifty hours to the day and been wide awake all the time—and he has so many future fortunes marked out for him that at three hundred and fifty years old his work will not be half done, and when at last all *is* finally accomplished, a minute dissection of his aged corpus will be necessary, that his earthly remains may be buried in all the places set down for him by these prophets.

But aside from a humorous contemplation of the subjects, he trusts he has done his work well; he is sure he has done it faithfully, and he honestly hopes that some good may come of his labors to write down here honestly the ignorance and imbecility of The Witches of New York.

THE END.

www.ingramcontent.com/pod-product-compliance
Lightning Source LLC
Chambersburg PA
CBHW071155160426
43196CB00011B/2090